SOLDIERS OF SARATOGA
★★★ COUNTY ★★★

Best wishes,

Paul Post

SOLDIERS OF SARATOGA COUNTY

★★★ COUNTY ★★★

FROM CONCORD TO KABUL

PAUL POST

Charleston · London

THE
History
PRESS

Published by The History Press
Charleston, SC 29403
www.historypress.net

First published 2010

Manufactured in the United States

ISBN 978.1.59629.009.9

Library of Congress Cataloging-in-Publication Data

Post, Paul.
Soldiers of Saratoga County : from Concord to Kabul / Paul Post.
p. cm.
ISBN 978-1-59629-009-9
1. Saratoga County (N.Y.)--History, Military. 2. Soldiers--New York (State)--Saratoga
County--Biography. 3. Saratoga County (N.Y.)--Biography. 4. Saratoga County (N.Y.)--
History, Local. I. Title.
F127.S26P67 2010
355.0092'274748--dc22
2010016598

To Harold and Frieda Post,
My parents

And to my true love Bonnie's parents,
Barbara and Lefty George

Four of the greatest generation's greatest

CONTENTS

CONTENTS

CONTENTS

WAR ON TERROR

ABOVE THE CALL OF DUTY

USS *SARATOGA*

FOREWORD

Soldiers of Saratoga County: From Concord to Kabul captures the true essence of this region's patriotic spirit while relating in detail the contributions that Saratoga County's sons and daughters have made to this great country of ours.

There are four different accounts—personal experiences—of Pearl Harbor Day alone.

I was surprised to learn how many different major engagements Saratoga County residents took part in, from Bunker Hill—the American Revolution's first major battle—to the current War on Terror.

Best of all, these stories are told through the eyes of those who were there and help readers understand the blood, sweat and tears that they shed and the sacrifices—financial, physical and emotional—that they made.

Few books I've read cover so many different time periods in American history, from the Revolution, the Civil War, the Indian campaigns, World Wars I and II, Korea and the Cold War to Vietnam and the current strife in Iraq and Afghanistan. Also, *Soldiers of Saratoga County* deals with people in all branches of the military—the army, navy, air force and marines.

It's surprising, too, to learn how many significant sites this region has that are related to our nation's military history, such as Saratoga National Historical Park, Stillwater; Grant's Cottage, Wilton; the New York State Military Museum, Saratoga Springs; and Rogers Island, Fort Edward.

As a veteran, a U.S. Naval Academy graduate and American Legion national commander for 2009/10, I encourage people of all ages to read *Soldiers of Saratoga County*. This collection of stories is sure to inspire everyone who reads it.

Clarence E. Hill, Captain (ret.), U.S. Navy
National Commander, American Legion, 2009/10

ACKNOWLEDGEMENTS

This project wouldn't have been possible without the support of *Saratogian* managing editor Barbara Lombardo. Pictures were taken by *Saratogian* photographers Erica Miller, Ed Burke and Rick Gargiulo.

Local town, city and county historians—too many to name—were of invaluable help. Their work is often taken for granted and goes unappreciated, but they nonetheless play an extremely important and overlooked role in preserving information for future generations' use and enjoyment.

Most of all, I want to thank every veteran, family member and others who were interviewed for their cooperation, interest and service to country and community.

INTRODUCTION

S aratoga County, New York, is home to one of the most historically significant sites in America: Saratoga National Historical Park, better known as Saratoga Battlefield, where Americans defeated and forced the surrender of British general John Burgoyne's army following the Battles of Saratoga on September 19 and October 7, 1777. Many historians consider this the turning point of the American Revolution.

Ever since then, Saratoga County's sons and daughters have been answering the call to duty whenever their country has needed them. This patriotism runs deep and has permeated generations of residents for nearly 250 years, affecting people from every town, village and hamlet in the county and surrounding area.

Soldiers of Saratoga County: From Concord to Kabul is a collection of roughly forty stories about the men and women who have not only served in the U.S. military but also have taken part in some of the most famous engagements in world history, from Bunker Hill, Pearl Harbor and Custer's Last Stand to D-Day and the current War on Terror. Most, but not all, of these stories have been previously published in *The Saratogian* newspaper, where I have worked since late 1995, and are the result of my writing about local veterans.

A handful of accounts are about people, such as Sonny Segan, Frank Copeland and the late Donald Porter, from neighboring Warren and Washington Counties. Likewise, two of the first pieces are about Rogers Island in Fort Edward, Washington County, and the lost radeau of Lake George, Warren County, both of which relate to the French and Indian War that preceded the American Revolution by roughly twenty years.

It was that war, between France and Great Britain, that decided control of the North American continent and set the stage for the Revolutionary War a couple of decades later. Few regions in America have such a dense concentration of historically significant military sites that relate to both of these wars. Likewise, while nearly every town in the United States has produced its share of veterans, few places rival the Saratoga area for having such a vast array of men and women who have served in virtually every war and fought in almost every major battle in American history.

They came not only from Saratoga Springs but also from the surrounding outlying towns and villages that crisscross the county from Corinth to Schuylerville and South Glens Falls to Clifton Park. It is my hope that *Soldiers of Saratoga County* will encourage readers to visit local sites that explain Saratoga County's role in American history, places such as the National Historical Park, Grant's Cottage in Wilton and the New York Military Museum in Saratoga Springs. Also, by putting these stories in book form, I have tried to create an educational resource that people can use to learn about vitally important events in American history, as told by the people who took part in them. Most importantly, I hope that readers will draw inspiration from these heroic U.S. service members and follow their example of building a better nation for future generations to enjoy.

SETTING THE STAGE

French and Indian War

ROGERS ISLAND: HISTORY UNEARTHED

Published June 9, 2007

Archaeologists led by Dr. David Starbuck have unearthed thousands of valuable military and Native American artifacts at Rogers Island in Fort Edward during the past few decades. When it comes to realizing the site's tourism potential, the town still hasn't scratched the surface.

In 1759, Fort Edward and Rogers Island were home to an estimated twenty thousand soldiers and support personnel, making it the third largest city in the colonies behind New York and Boston. There were no bloody conflicts there, but the fort played a crucial role in the struggle between Great Britain and France for control of the North American continent during the French and Indian War.

"Around Fort Edward you dig a shovel and you don't know what you're going to come up with," said Eileen Hannay, manager of the Rogers Island Visitors Center, which has attracted people from fourteen countries and every state but Hawaii since its opening six years ago.

The original Fort Edward, built in 1755, was located on the east bank of the river directly across from Rogers Island, where numerous barracks and three hospitals were situated. The military site extended to the river's west bank in Moreau, Saratoga County, where one of only two royal blockhouses in the country once stood.

"This is as far north as you could go on the Hudson River," Hannay said. "Then you had to go overland."

A military road connected Fort Edward to Fort William Henry in Lake George, where major events in the French and Indian War occurred 250 years ago this summer. The British held both forts and lost the northern one following a bloody six-day siege that began on August 3, 1757, made famous by James Fenimore Cooper's *Last of the Mohicans*.

"When the siege [began] they could hear cannon, muskets and small guns here in Fort Edward," Hannay said. "They didn't have all the background noise we do today. They knew right off that the fort was being attacked, even before messengers went back and forth."

Unlike Fort William Henry and Fort Ticonderoga on Lake Champlain, Fort Edward was never attacked, although it's believed that the French could have moved farther south and taken it without much trouble. Its relatively peaceful existence helps explain why it has never garnered the same degree of attention as other outposts.

"In history, we tend to place importance on places where battles were fought," Hannay said.

Rogers Island got its name from Major Robert Rogers, who, in October 1757, wrote "Rules of Ranging" detailing guerrilla-style combat techniques for woodland settings. His outfit, Rogers Rangers, is considered the forerunner of today's modern-day Special Forces.

After capturing Fort William Henry, the French burned it. The next year (1758), the British tried to mount a northward attack that failed miserably. In 1759, they amassed sixteen thousand regular and provincial soldiers at Fort Edward in preparation for an assault on Fort Carillon (Ticonderoga). With families, settlers and doctors mixed in, there were an estimated twenty thousand people at Fort Edward.

Four years later, the war ended, and the fort was evacuated in 1769. It was used only as barracks during the American Revolution.

"By the 1800s they were building houses on top of it," Hannay said. "The original fort encompassed three streets in modern Fort Edward."

There have been several major excavations in and around Fort Edward, and more than ninety thousand artifacts—from Native American points to clay pipes, musket balls and military uniform buttons—have been recovered.

In 2009, the nineteenth annual Adirondack Community College Archaeological Field School focused on a sutler's house built by a civilian merchant during the French and Indian War to sell goods to the British soldiers stationed at Fort Edward.

"This place is an archaeological treasure," said Lynn Hohmann, a volunteer worker. "It helps you understand who we are and where we came from. It's a living history museum."

BENEATH LAKE GEORGE: THE LOST RADEAU

Published January 23, 2006

After documenting one of America's most famous shipwrecks, historians are now sharing their findings in a new documentary movie, *The Lost Radeau*.

Joseph Zarzynski of Wilton, an underwater archaeologist, told about this sunken Lake George warship that dates to the French and Indian War. Dubbed the "land tortoise" because of its unique shape, the radeau rests in 107 feet of forty-five-degree water about two miles from the lake's southern end.

"This is the only vessel in the lake that's a true time capsule," Zarzynski said. "A time capsule is something that hasn't changed. We sometimes forget about the history that's down there."

He and a team of fellow explorers happened upon the fifty-two- by eighteen-foot boat while scanning the lake bottom with sonar on June 26, 1990. In 1998, it was designated a National Historic Landmark, one of only six ships with such status, including the battleships *Utah* and *Arizona* at Pearl Harbor and the Civil War ironclad *Monitor* off the coast of North Carolina.

"And no one's ever heard of it," Zarzynski said.

The British built the radeau in 1758 near the site of present-day Million Dollar Beach in Lake George. It was a floating gun battery with an oak hull and pine bulwarks designed to deflect musket fire.

With thirteen holes for rowing and seven cannons, the flat-bottomed boat could get close to shore to support amphibious landings. Its artillery would clear out enemy forces and pave the way for troops to reach shore, similar to the role that battleships played at Normandy on D-Day.

In 1758, in the midst of the French and Indian War, the British hoped to drive the French from Fort Carillon (Ticonderoga) at the south end of Lake Champlain. Lake George was the easiest way to get soldiers and munitions up there.

The British were repulsed in July 1758, despite far outnumbering their opponents. Following their retreat to Lake George, the British built the radeau, intending to use it in a later campaign.

"It never got up there," Zarzynski said.

On October 22, 1758, the British sunk the boat, hoping they could raise it the following year for use during another attack. Many boats were sunk before winter, in twenty to thirty feet of water, to keep French raiders from burning them.

Unfortunately, the radeau went to unanticipated depths. The next year, 1759, the British under Lord Jeffrey Amherst succeeded in driving the French out.

"These warships were pretty much forgotten," Zarzynski said.

The radeau, except for minor damage, is completely intact, making it the only original ship of its kind in existence. Zarzynski, Dave Van Aken of Clifton Park and Bob Benway of Queensbury were the first three divers to visit the site. Since then, more than four hundred others have done the same. The shipwreck is marked by buoys as a New York State Submerged Heritage Preserve.

Divers are discouraged from going inside the boat because the 250-year-old pine is so fragile that air bubbles cause it to flake off.

"We're worried about the acceleration of deterioration of this vessel," Zarzynski said.

A portion of sales from *The Lost Radeau* will be used to create a fund designed to ensure the boat's future protection.

For more information see www.thelostradeau.com.

BATEAUX BELOW: NATIONAL RECOGNITION

Published August 14, 2009

The White House has recognized a local organization for its extensive efforts at protecting underwater historic resources in Lake George. Bateaux Below, headquartered in Wilton, has been awarded a Preserve America Steward designation, a distinction given to only two recipients nationwide.

The honor recognizes Bateaux Below and its volunteers for their exemplary efforts, especially at maintaining a state-administered shipwreck park for scuba divers called Submerged Heritage Preserves. The site opened in 1993 and was the first of its kind in the state. "It's going to help shine light on the submerged cultural resources and show their importance," said Joseph Zarzynski of Wilton, the group's executive director.

Bateaux Below has spent the last twenty-two years studying the lake's shipwrecks and implementing programs that promote their historic preservation. The Preserve America Steward award recognizes the efforts of Bateaux Below's eleven volunteers: Dr. Russell Bellico, Bob Benway, Vince Capone, Terry Crandall, John Farrell, Steven C. Resler, Peter Pepe, Paul Cornell, Elinor Mossop, Dr. Sam Bowser and Zarzynski.

This year (2009) marks the 250th anniversary of the raising of the Sunken Fleet of 1758, which the British, under Amherst, used to drive the French from Fort Carillon (Ticonderoga) in 1759, during the French and Indian War. The British, although possessing far superior forces, were repulsed in their attempt to capture Fort Carillon in 1758.

Returning to Lake George, they sank more than 260 boats, rather than have them fall into French hands. The next year, they raised about 200 of the vessels, launched another attack with twelve thousand soldiers and won.

Historians still aren't sure how the British raised the sunken boats, but about forty to fifty remain on the lake bottom, including a rare "land tortoise" (radeau) that has been designated a National Historic Landmark. The remaining boats are ones that might have been damaged and left behind as the British tried to find ways to raise the Sunken Fleet.

"It's amazing what they were able to do," Zarzynski said. "Whether they used block and tackle, or brute force, it shows their toughness and ability to do an extremely difficult job."

AMERICAN REVOLUTION

EDWARD BEVINS: BUNKER HILL DRUMMER BOY

Published January 25, 2009

Edward Bevins was just sixteen when he joined the New Hampshire militia as a private. Two months later, on June 16, 1775, he found himself fighting against the British in the Battle of Bunker Hill—the first major engagement of the American Revolution.

Bevins, of Lyndeborough, had signed on as a drummer boy but turned the drum in for a rifle in the quest for America's freedom and independence. He spent three years in the military before his discharge in August 1778. Two years later, he moved to Wilton in the vicinity of the former Louden Church. While seated around a fireplace, he would often tell his children and grandchildren his first-person account of the Battle of Bunker Hill.

"After we had laid down our drums and fifes, we drummer boys began making it hot for the British Red Coats," Bevins told listeners, as recorded in Evelyn Barrett Britten's book, *Chronicles of Saratoga*. "They charged us again and again, but we drove them back. Veterans of the British army, well-trained and with the most modern guns and all the ammunition they could carry, they outmatched us in numbers."

The Americans' objective at Bunker Hill was to foil the British attempt to get a foothold around Boston.

"That was the first real battle of the Revolution," said Terrence M. Vaughan, a Boston National Historical Park ranger. "Lexington and Concord (two months earlier in April) was really just a skirmish. Lexington and Concord was a terrible blow to the British army's soldierly pride. They were beaten back to Boston by peasants."

The Continental army, if it could be called that, was little more than a collection of town militias. Soldiers from Connecticut, Massachusetts and New Hampshire gathered in Cambridge to prepare for the march to Charlestown, the site of Bunker Hill. The British, in contrast, had the best-trained army in the world and outnumbered the Americans nearly three to one, with no shortage of ammunition or supplies.

George Washington, named commander in chief of the Continental army, couldn't get to Boston in time. In his stead, Artemis Ward was in charge.

Dr. Joseph Warren, for whom Warren County, New York, is named, was president of the Provincial Congress, and Colonel William Prescott, from the town of Pepperell, led the march to Charlestown, directly across from Boston.

The British were clad in heavy wool uniforms, and with their muskets, sacks, blankets, food and accoutrements, they carried about sixty-seven pounds in addition to their body weight. On the American side, only Connecticut's troops wore any kind of uniform.

"The rest of the New England militiamen wore their best working clothes—breeches, wide-brimmed hats, loose-fitting shifts, vests and coats," Vaughan said. "As it was quite warm, I'm sure they laid these vest and coats aside. In the final assault, the British troops made themselves a lot lighter by casting aside much of their baggage. The first assault began about 2:30 [p.m.] and the battle was over by four thirty or five o'clock."

The Patriots retreated back to Cambridge and Medford.

"But the British did not pursue us," Bevins would tell listeners.

The British loss was 226 officers and men killed, 828 wounded, while we lost 145 dead or missing, with 304 wounded. The battle became a real victory for us; for we had now seen the superior numbers of the best-trained troops waver before our attack. Thus, the battle became a great moral victory for us.

We were mostly country boys, who had quickly assembled but were matching the British man for man. Our guns were old flintlock fowling pieces, which some of us had used at home to hunt for rabbits. Something inside of the boys seemed to give them strength and courage of superhuman quality.

We feared nothing. Many of my friends fell at my side and were bayoneted like hogs are slaughtered at the killing time. As a drummer, I was not considered a fighting man but I fought that day, believe me! Now and then I was able to look back toward the nearest houses, steeples of churches and the shrouds of ships in the harbor.

It seemed there were thousands watching the battle and how they cheered each time we drove the charging Red Coats back. Then it was we drummer boys, with shovels, who filled the hogsheads with sand and waited for the enemy.

As they neared the top with their bayonets ready for our hearts, we topped over the heavy barrels of sand and away they went rolling down the hill, gathering speed as they rolled. They struck the solidly packed Red Coats just below their knees, breaking many of their legs and tossing them on top of one another like firewood.

Before they could pull themselves out of their mess, we were scampering away and were able to escape, letting them have the hill. Prescott gave the order of our retreat, which was harassed by a withering fire from the British ships and batteries.

A Patriot Comes Home

Bevins was born on April 8, 1759, and joined the militia in Concord, New Hampshire. He is listed in historical records as fighting at Bunker Hill in Spaulding's company of Reed's Regiment. He would march with three different companies before his eventual discharge.

In Wilton, he and his wife, Mary, had a son, Edward, and daughter, Polly, who married Jason Adams on January 8, 1801. Their son, Lewis, inherited the Bevins homestead and lived there until 1880.

Bevins died on January 8, 1821, just shy of his sixty-second birthday. His stories about Bunker Hill were kept alive by his descendants for years to come, passed from one generation to the next.

He is buried at Wilton's Louden Cemetery on Louden Road, just east of the intersection with Ingersol Road. The exact location of his grave is uncertain, but it's believed that he's buried near his son, daughter and grandchildren.

A grandson, also named Jason Adams, fought in the Civil War. His Louden Cemetery grave is identified with a GAR (Grand Army of the Republic) marker.

Bunker Hill Controversy Continues

Today, it's generally accepted that the Battle of Bunker Hill wasn't fought there at all but at nearby Breed's Hill. Vaughan, however, thinks otherwise.

"Fifty years after the battle, Daniel Webster and General Lafayette, with over one hundred veterans of the battle, came to lay the cornerstone of the monument and consistently referred to the site upon which they stood as Bunker Hill," he said.

> *The controversy over Bunker versus Breeds goes back to a gentleman by the name of Richard Frothingham, a Charlestown historian who lived right across from the monument at No. 9 Monument Square. In 1875, he gave a discourse to distinguished members of the Massachusetts Historical Society at which he exhibited maps and documents pertaining to the battle.*

He displayed the oldest map of Charlestown that could be found, which included Boston, the harbor and harbor islands. It also showed rebel entrenchments and the battle formation of the British regulars on June 17, 1775. The map was made right after the battle by a British officer named Page but was based on a survey of the area presumably done earlier by a Captain Montresor.

"The hill in Charlestown upon which the rebel redoubt sits is labeled 'Bunker Hill' and the higher elevation beyond it is labeled quite clearly 'Breeds Hill,'" Vaughan said.

> *After praising the cartographic skills of Page, and by inference Montresor, Frothingham states in his discourse that they had it mixed up. He cites as his only evidence old deeds he had seen of Charlestown property which refer to the higher elevation as Bunker Hill. He states that no mention is ever made of a Breeds Hill. However, he never mentions where he had seen these deeds, nor are there any copies in the exhibit.*
>
> *The British seemed to know quite clearly that there were two hills with two distinct names. They labeled the higher elevation Breeds Hill and the lower elevation Bunker Hill. After the battle, the sides seemed to refer to the location of the battle as Bunker or Bunker's Hill and, in all reports of the battle, it was referred to as "The Battle of Bunker Hill."*
>
> *As far as I am concerned, it is Bunker Hill. I am convinced the British were correct. Frothingham, with scant evidence, came along one hundred years after the battle and said they were all wrong.*

But Frothingham was held in high esteem by members of the Massachusetts Historical Society and seems to have won the day.

"Many years ago, a bronze plaque was put outside the monument labeling the hill 'Breeds,' upon which the Battle of Bunker Hill was actually fought,"

Vaughan said. "It has led to much confusion. But, then again, there was confusion before the battle, during the battle, after the battle and confusion ever since."

Regardless of its name, the battle contributed to the Americans' goal of driving the British out of Boston. "There were no more major engagements that summer," Vaughan said. "The British had lots of wounds to lick, so to speak, and retrenched on the Boston peninsula."

Then it got colder. The British army was not prepared to fight in winter. It was during those long, cold months that American colonel Henry Knox brought cannons overland from Fort Ticonderoga to Boston.

On the morning of March 5, 1776, the British awoke to see the American fortifications at Dorchester Heights. "Without a fight, they evacuated Boston on March 17, 1776," Vaughan said. "It was Washington's first strategic victory. New England was liberated."

COLONEL SIDNEY BERRY: AIDE TO GENERAL WASHINGTON

Previously unpublished

Among Northumberland's many Patriots, two brothers-in-law deserve special recognition for their valor during the Revolution and importance to the town's early settlement.

Thomas Thompson came to Northumberland from New Jersey about 1781 with his wife, Elizabeth, and her brother, Colonel Sidney Berry, whose historic house still stands on the west bank of the Hudson River, about five miles south of Fort Edward. It is located on West River Road near Crocker Reef.

Recently, the house was owned by the late noted philanthropist Alfred Z. Solomon but was sold in November 2005 for $1.5 million.

West River Road was built for military purposes by Lord Loudon in autumn 1756, during the French and Indian War, and led from what is now Schuylerville to the Block House, then standing on the west bank of the river opposite Fort Edward.

Thompson's house was farther back from the river and is now gone. Thompson was in the New Jersey militia from 1778 to 1780, recruited by Berry for the Hunterdon County Fourth Regiment in 1778. Upon moving to Saratoga County, Thompson continued his Revolutionary War service as a private in Captain Jacob Vosburgh's company, belonging to the Seventeenth Albany County Regiment of New York State Militia commanded by William Bradford Whiting.

Berry was born on June 30, 1745, in Monmouth County, New Jersey, and during the Revolution had been an aide to General George Washington himself.

In 1776, while the Continental Congress was drafting the Declaration of Independence, ships landed in New York Harbor carrying the largest expeditionary force that Great Britain had ever sent overseas. The armada unloaded twenty-seven well-trained British regiments and eight thousand Hessian mercenaries—a total force of thirty-two thousand.

Washington's ill-equipped, poorly trained American army numbered nineteen thousand. Its presence was a source of amusement to the brothers Lord Richard Howe, admiral of the fleet, and General William Howe, newly appointed commander of land forces in America.

On the day after publication of the Declaration of Independence in New York, Lord Howe sent a note under a flag of truce to Washington. Colonel Reed, Washington's adjutant, met the British party and was given an envelope addressed to "George Washington, Esq. New York." The letter did not identify Washington as a general or commander of American forces.

The British boat's captain said, as he handed it over, "I have a letter sir from Lord Howe to Mr. Washington."

"Sir," Reed replied, "we have no person in our army with that address," and he refused to accept the letter.

Four days later, Howe sent a staff officer to confer with Washington, again asking him to accept a letter addressed to "George Washington," which Washington steadfastly refused.

On August 30, following the Battle of Long Island, Lord Howe once again tried to send a communication to Washington without recognizing his rank. This time, Washington sent Berry, his commissary officer, to receive the messenger with the reply that he would not negotiate with Howe, that being the prerogative of Congress.

Several days later, however, Congress sent Benjamin Franklin, John Adams and Edward Rutledge to confer with General and Lord Howe at the general's Staten Island headquarters, representing the Free and Independent States of America.

Howe said that he "felt for America as for a brother and if America should fall [I] should feel and lament it like the loss of a brother."

Franklin replied, "My Lord, we will do our utmost endeavors to save your lordship that mortification."

Upon moving upstate, and after the Revolution, Berry became one of the Saratoga area's most prominent citizens. In 1798, he was elected Northumberland's first town supervisor when it separated from the Town of Saratoga. Before that, he had been Saratoga's road commissioner as early as 1789.

Berry helped organize a local school district and was appointed one of the first public school commissioners in Saratoga in 1796 and 1797. That district had teachers and students who rose to great distinction in life. John W. Taylor would serve in Congress for twenty-two years and was Speaker of the House for two terms. Silas Wright became governor of New York and a U.S. senator. Taylor Lewis became a professor at Union College, and Seth E. Sill was a New York Supreme Court justice.

In addition to his roles in government and education, Berry was the first surrogate judge to serve on the Court of Common Pleas or General Sessions, serving from February 1791, when it was organized in Saratoga County, to September 1794. He was a member of the New York State Assembly, representing Albany County in 1790 and Saratoga County in 1791 and 1792. He was a member of the first board of trustees of Washington Academy in Salem, appointed in 1791.

He and Thompson started one of the first temperance societies in New York State in Saratoga, and Thompson is listed as the organization's treasurer in 1808.

General Samuel Lewis, a neighbor from Moreau, knew Colonel Berry well and described him as follows:

> *I can see him now—the old-fashioned gentleman—dressed in short breeches with silver knee and shoe buckles. I remember how I stood in reverential awe of him, notwithstanding he was full of anecdote, cheerful and kind.*

Sources: History of Washington County, New York *(1904, vol. 1) and the* Moreau Sun.

REVOLUTIONARY WAR CHRISTMAS: FROM SARATOGA TO VALLEY FORGE

Published December 25, 2008

Many of the eight thousand American Patriots who helped win the Battles of Saratoga in September and October 1777 spent a bleak Christmas that winter at Valley Forge. In fact, most had come from New England and didn't even celebrate Christmas because their Puritan heritage rejected the drunken revelry that surrounded the holiday back in Europe, a holiday they viewed as pagan.

About 450 Patriots died fighting the British at Saratoga, considered the turning point of the Revolution. At Valley Forge, disease and poor diet proved even more lethal as nearly 2,000 Americans succumbed without a shot being fired—more casualties than in any Revolutionary War battle.

"Nobody dies from starvation," said William Lange, a Valley Forge park ranger. "They died because there wasn't a sufficient enough freeze to kill the sources of disease. Plus, they were lacking supplies to combat the cold."

The two Battles of Saratoga were fought on September 19 and October 7, 1777. Following General John Burgoyne's surrender, most of the British were marched to Boston, where they spent the winter under guard.

"The American militia would have gone home," said Joseph Craig, a Saratoga National Historical Park ranger. "Most were from Massachusetts, New Hampshire, Connecticut. They had been called out by their governors. If you weren't in the Continental army, you were expected to be in the militia."

Continental regulars, however, got marching orders to join General George Washington's army at Valley Forge, Pennsylvania, the site he'd chosen to keep watch of British-occupied Philadelphia, which the redcoats had taken control of in October. Two other positions had been considered—Wilmington, Delaware, and a line from Lancaster to Reading, Pennsylvania.

Only one other American general favored Valley Forge, but Washington could see its advantages.

"It was well-situated with natural defenses, and they could block roadways from the west to keep the British from getting supplies," Lange said.

Traveling by foot, soldiers from Saratoga arrived at Valley Forge in mid-December. With no housing, most lived in tents or Indian-style shelters.

"Conditions were pretty miserable," said Mark Brier, a Valley Forge ranger. "One of the first things they [did was] start building cabins. Once they got those built, they were a little better off."

Christmas, for the most part, was just another day.

The surrounding Pennsylvania countryside, however, had been settled largely by Germans, who had a variety of rich Christmas traditions, including the *Tannenbaum*, or Christmas tree.

"They would decorate with greenery, which is considered symbolic of the continuance of life," Lange said. "They had ornamentation and fruit.

I'm sure some of those people who were here in the village of Valley Forge and nearby farms would have celebrated, but it was not a celebration for the army. Basically, it all depends upon where the soldiers come from."

One year earlier, the German practice of celebrating Christmas had contributed to one of America's greatest Revolutionary War victories. Washington, after crossing the Delaware River on Christmas Day 1776, took the British-allied German Hessians by surprise at Trenton.

"One of the reasons they were able to surprise them the way they did was because they were celebrating that holiday," Lange said.

The American triumph inspired many new recruits to join the Patriot cause and helped retain those already serving whose enlistments were due to expire.

"That Christmas was a major time in Revolutionary War history," Lange said.

Back north, in the region surrounding Saratoga, Christmas 1777 probably came and went without much fanfare.

"The war had trashed the area, houses were burned out," Craig said. "If people were doing anything, it was probably rebuilding. There wasn't much celebration. Christmas was not a big, big holiday by any means compared to today."

Many of the customs most commonly associated with Christmas in America weren't adopted until the nineteenth-century Victorian era. Ironically, English author Charles Dickens is quite often credited with "inventing" the holiday as it is known today.

The Dutch, of course, had first settled what is now New York, including the Hudson Valley, and their traditions included the Feast of St. Nicholas, who became the model for *Sinterklaas*, also known as Santa Claus.

No one at Valley Forge, however, awoke to find wrapped gifts outside their tents or freezing cold cabins.

"Basically, for most of the army, it was a day of work," Craig said.

The twelve thousand soldiers and five hundred women and children camp followers weren't prepared for what faced them. They were living in close quarters with poor sanitation, and disease claimed two thousand lives as winter wore on.

The army's numbers fluctuated greatly because some Continental soldiers were allowed home on furlough while the enlistments of many others expired. At one point, the force was less than half its original size.

One of the most significant developments at Valley Forge was the arrival of Baron Friedrich Wilhelm von Steuben, a Prussian-German army officer who is credited with teaching the Continental army the essentials of military drill and discipline.

Von Steuben wrote the book that became the standard United States drill manual and served as Washington's chief of staff during the final years of the Revolution. He arrived at Valley Forge in late February and began whipping the Americans into shape as a fine-tuned fighting unit. Equally important, he established sanitation and camp layouts that set the standard for the next 150 years.

Under von Steuben's direction, the Americans spent the entire spring marching and training at Valley Forge. The fruits of their hard work paid off at the Battle of Barren Hill on May 20, 1778, and again at the Battle of Monmouth.

Thanks to the American victory at Saratoga—and Benjamin Franklin's diplomatic efforts—France decided to help the United States in its war against Britain. The British didn't want to lose New York, so they began evacuating Philadelphia on June 18, 1778, sending a force of eleven thousand troops northward with a twelve-mile-long baggage train.

Washington's Continental army left Valley Forge in pursuit and, after careful deliberation, decided to attack the British at Monmouth on June 28, 1778. Fighting in one-hundred-degree temperatures, heatstroke claimed almost as many men as the combat.

During the night, the British escaped and eventually made it to New York. Technically, the battle was a draw, but the Americans could claim victory on two fronts. First, they were still in the field while the British continued their move northward. Second, the Patriots had withstood a major engagement using von Steuben's newly instilled tactics.

Following the 1777 Battles of Saratoga, Christmas would come and go four times before the Americans finally won their hard-fought struggle for independence, culminating with the 1781 Battle of Yorktown.

"It was a long, expensive, heartbreaking war," Craig said. "There wasn't a lot of reason to celebrate."

CIVIL WAR

CORINTH'S FIGHTING WALKER FAMILY

Published March 29, 2009

Alexander Walker was forty-nine when he and his three sons joined the Union army on October 20, 1861.

They were among the 129 men, 20 of whom died from wounds or disease, who enlisted from Corinth during the Civil War.

The next year, Walker fell at Antietam while carrying the Stars and Stripes alongside his sons—David, Romaine and Epaphroditas—who later joined an elite cavalry unit with which they fought for the duration of the war.

"They reenlisted to avenge their father's death," town historian Rachel Clothier said. "The brothers served the rest of the war and were not killed."

The Civil War affected small towns like Corinth emotionally and financially, and no place could escape its devastating impacts as word of killed and wounded filtered home from gruesome battlefields. The Town of Corinth paid needy families $1.50 to $3.00 per week, and Nathan Wells Buckmaster, who owned a general store, gave a barrel of flour to the families of every man in the war.

Alexander, Epaphroditas and Romaine were sawyers, while David was a carpenter. Together, they joined the Thirtieth Regiment at a simple Main Street recruiting station.

"Someone from the army would come to town, set up in a general store—a barrel with a board on top—and encourage men to enlist," Clothier said.

Corinth's Civil War recruiting station was in the building that later became Allen's Auto Supply (since demolished), on the east side of Main

Street, between the current-day Rocco's Pizza and Corinth Wine & Liquor. It was one of the oldest buildings on Main Street at the time.

The Walkers fought together at the Second Battle of Bull Run (August 29, 1862), at South Mountain (September 14, 1862) and at Antietam (September 17, 1862)—the bloodiest single-day battle in American history, with twenty-three thousand casualties. Alexander became a color sergeant, making him an easy target, and his bullet-riddled body remained on the field at Antietam, where he is buried in the New York section, seventh row, grave no. 643.

Antietam was the first major battle fought on Northern soil. After winning the Second Battle of Bull Run, Robert E. Lee's strategy was to seek new supplies and recruits from the border state of Maryland, which had considerable pockets of Confederate sympathizers, and to affect public opinion prior to the upcoming elections in the North.

Despite being outnumbered two to one, Lee's Army of Northern Virginia fought the Union Army of the Potomac, under Major General George McClellan, to a standstill. Lee's invasion into Maryland, however, was ended, and President Lincoln felt that there was enough of a victory to announce his Emancipation Proclamation. Also, the battle's outcome discouraged the British and French governments from recognizing the Confederacy.

Lincoln traveled to Antietam two weeks after the battle and spent four days talking to McClellan, touring the battlefield and visiting the wounded on both sides.

The battle-scarred Thirtieth Regiment was mustered out in 1863, but the Walker brothers decided to rejoin on August 23, 1864, as members of the battle-tested Second New York Veterans Cavalry. They later fought in the Red River Campaign in Louisiana, and Epaphroditas kept his mother informed with a number of letters from the Deep South. He expressed amazing confidence about his fate, considering what had befallen his late father.

"It is with pleasure that I now answer your kind letter," he wrote. "I'm glad to hear that all is well. We are all well at present. It is not in my lot to be killed here. Kiss all the children for me."

In one account, he described chasing Rebel soldiers.

"When we draw our old cheese knives they get up and get," he declared. "We run them two miles and they got away from us. But we got one of them. Romaine fired four shots at them. It was fun to chase them."

On one occasion, he detailed the goods and supplies they captured: forty horses, fifty mules, twenty-one bales of cotton, wagons, five carts and hens and hogs, which they ate.

The Red River Campaign consisted of a series of battles fought along the Red River from March 10 to May 22, 1864. It was a Union initiative, fought between thirty thousand Union troops under the command of Major General Nathaniel P. Banks and Confederate troops under the command of Major General Richard Taylor, whose strength varied from six thousand to twelve thousand.

The Union had three objectives: (1) destroy the Confederate army commanded by Taylor; (2) confiscate as much as 100,000 bales of cotton from plantations along the Red River; and (3) capture Shreveport, Louisiana Confederate headquarters for the Trans-Mississippi Department, control the Red River to the north and occupy east Texas. Union strategists in Washington thought that the occupation of east Texas and control of the Red River would separate Texas from the rest of the Confederacy. Texas was the source of much-needed guns, food and supplies for Confederate troops.

There was also some concern that the twenty-five thousand French troops in Mexico sent by Napoleon III and under the command of Emperor Maximilian might join forces with Confederate troops in Texas and use the Red River Valley as a point of entry to reinforce Confederate troops in the Trans-Mississippi Department. This latter fear proved to be unfounded but was thought to be a factor considered by Union general in chief Henry W. Halleck, as well as President Lincoln, in planning the campaign.

It turned out to be a dismal failure, characterized by poor planning and mismanagement, in which not a single objective was fully accomplished. Taylor's successful defense of the Red River Valley with a smaller force is considered one of the most brilliant Confederate military accomplishments of the war.

A Town of Corinth sesquicentennial (1968) publication authored by Arthur Eggleston identifies Philip Rice as Corinth's first native son to enlist in the Civil War. His comrades elected him second lieutenant in the Thirtieth Regiment. He was killed on August 29, 1862, while leading his company in the Second Battle of Bull Run, which—like First Bull Run—the Confederates won.

From there, the fighting shifted to South Mountain, where Lee's army, although heavily outnumbered, delayed McClellan's advance for a day before withdrawing.

Three days later, the armies met again at Antietam.

Of the Corinth residents who died during the war, four men, including John Fenn and John Herrick, perished in Southern prison camps. Private Charles Davis died at Libby Prison in Richmond, and Private Sylvanus Densmore, captured in Florida, starved to death at Georgia's infamous Andersonville Prison.

Corinth was represented in almost every major battle of the war. Afterward, a local branch of the Grand Army of the Republic was formed and called Philip Rice Post No. 290 in honor of the first enlistee. The group was organized by Captain Ambrose Clothier Hickok, who fought in several bitter campaigns and was among the guards stationed outside Ford's Theatre in Washington, D.C., the night Lincoln was assassinated. He was also a guard on the funeral train that carried the president back to Illinois.

For many years, Corinth's Civil War veterans would tell stories about their battlefield experiences. Ransford H. Densmore carried a constant reminder, the result of being wounded in the head at the Battle of Hanover Courthouse in Virginia. It's said that he was unconscious for about three weeks.

The last of Corinth's Union soldiers died in the 1930s, among them Thomas Herrick and Thomas Peak. Myron King, age ninety-four, was the last remaining veteran at the time of his death on August 12, 1937.

UNKNOWN SOLDIER COMES HOME

Published September 4, 2009

A New York Civil War soldier, killed 147 years ago in America's bloodiest battle, is finally coming home.

In October 2008, a hiker at Antietam National Battlefield Park in Maryland discovered bone fragments and artifacts that sparked an extensive archaeological excavation, followed by testing at the Smithsonian Institute in Washington, D.C.

Uniform buttons clearly identify the soldier as a New York volunteer, and plans call for burial with full military honors at Gerald B. Solomon Saratoga National Cemetery on September 17, the battle's anniversary. Services will be preceded by ceremonies at the New York State Military Museum in Saratoga Springs.

"Here's a man who came here 147 years ago; he never got to go home," Antietam Park superintendent John Howard said. "Every soldier deserves to go home. This young man is no different. These are men who made the ultimate sacrifice. They gave the full measure of devotion for their beliefs."

Through jawbone tests, officials believe the soldier was between seventeen and twenty-one years old at the time of his death. His identity, regiment and place of residence remain a mystery.

The Union had far superior numbers at Antietam, eighty-seven thousand to the Confederates' thirty-six thousand, and although both sides lost equal numbers, the Union claimed victory because it held the field when fighting finally

Above: A U.S. waist belt plate was among the items found with the remains of an unknown soldier at Antietam National Battlefield.

Left: Hundreds of people, including Civil War–era reenactors, turned out for ceremonies for an unknown Union soldier who was reinterred at Gerald B.H. Solomon Saratoga National Ceremony on September 17, 2009.

An unknown Union Civil War soldier, killed at Antietam on September 17, 1862, was reinterred with full military honors at Gerald B.H. Solomon Saratoga National Cemetery on September 17, 2009.

ceased. The battle, on September 17, 1862, was a virtual bloodbath, as more than twenty-three thousand were killed or wounded in twelve hours of carnage.

"A lot of people ask, 'Is anything worth that kind of sacrifice?'" Howard said. "We refer to Antietam as the day America changed, because two weeks later Lincoln issued a preliminary Emancipation Proclamation. That led us down the road to freedom for all men, and now, in 2009, we have the first African American president."

In no uncertain terms, the American civil rights movement was born at Antietam, the day thousands gave their lives. More importantly, at the time, Lincoln's proclamation opened the doors for African Americans to join the Union cause. About 200,000 black soldiers, from New England residents to escaped Southern slaves, took up arms and helped decide the war's outcome.

The unknown New York soldier's remains were discovered in an area called Miller's Cornfield, where fighting took place from 5:45 to 9:00 a.m. "The Union, in charge of the field, buried soldiers where they fell or close to it," Howard said. "In 1865 and '66, they were moved to our National Cemetery here. Basically, they just missed him."

The grave was never found because the soldier was buried near a limestone outcropping, called a fin, which farmers would have avoided when plowing. Nearly a century and a half later, the hiker spotted bone fragment and a button in soil around a woodchuck hole.

Excavation revealed other artifacts—more buttons, a buckle and leather from shoes or a belt that the soldier was wearing that day. National Park Service archaeologist Stephen R. Potter prepared a briefing statement about the finds—three New York State Excelsior buttons, four U.S. general service buttons and two New York state cuff buttons from the left sleeve. "The two New York cuff buttons tell us that this was a New York State–issued coat or jacket and not a federal issue," Potter wrote.

The fact that four New York Excelsior buttons had been replaced by four U.S. general service buttons leads researchers to believe that the soldier was part of a veteran regiment that had seen hard campaigning.

Archaeologists also found six tin-washed, four-hole iron trouser buttons, used to attach suspender straps.

"The dark stain of the lower portion of a leather suspender strap and a badly corroded iron suspender adjuster were recorded in the field," Potter wrote. "A U.S. waist belt plate, with oval studs on the back (the so-called puppy-paw back, an early war issue) was still attached to a portion of the leather belt, which the brass front of the buckle helped to preserve by precipitating cupric salts into the soil surrounding it."

Only pieces of bone, not the entire skeletal remains, were recovered. Forensics determined that the young man was suffering from a severely impacted wisdom tooth.

"He had to be in agony aside from the fear of battle," Howard said.

Additional analysis called a Prior test might tell if the soldier was a recent immigrant or what part of Europe his ancestors were from.

All remains and artifacts will be placed in a small box made from walnut grown on the battlefield. "Those are things he was wearing; they should be buried with him," Howard said.

A New York Military Forces Honor Guard is slated to visit Antietam on September 15, where the walnut repository will be placed in a simple pine casket, typical of the Civil War period. Remains will be brought to Saratoga Springs on September 16 and will lie in repose at the military museum for public viewing prior to burial with full military honors at Gerald B.H. Solomon Saratoga National Cemetery in Stillwater.

"We get three-quarters of a million visitors here each year," Howard said. "We tell them, don't try to picture thousands. Just picture one soldier, what they went through."

More than five hundred people turned out for burial services at Gerald B.H. Solomon Saratoga National Cemetery on September 17, 2009. A brief essay about the unknown soldier serves as the epilogue to Soldiers of Saratoga County.

GREENRIDGE CEMETERY: CIVIL WAR HONOR ROLL

Published May 25, 2009

Some died on the battlefield, and some lived another seventy years, enjoying the freedom they fought for during the War Between the States.

Throughout Saratoga County, hundreds of graves mark the final resting place of heroes who preserved the Union by sacrificing everything they had—fortunes, futures, lives—in the Civil War.

The Spa City's Greenridge Cemetery is the final resting place of many figures of distinction, such as Private David Price, who served in the Fifty-fourth Massachusetts Volunteer Infantry Regiment, the nearly all-black unit depicted in the 1989 movie *Glory*, starring Matthew Broderick as its white commander, Colonel Robert Gould Shaw.

Civil War historian Lance Ingmire displays a blow-up poster of a soldier buried at Greenridge Cemetery in Saratoga Springs.

"The most famous engagement the Fifty-fourth Massachusetts was involved in was the attack on Fort Wagner, South Carolina, on July 18, 1863," said Mark Bodnar of Loudonville, a Civil War historian and author. "No doubt Private Price was with the regiment during this attack."

The coastal fort was a Confederate stronghold that the Union needed to take in order to keep Rebel forces from firing on ships.

"A lot of guys from New York City joined up with the Fifty-fourth," Bodnar said. "I think Albany had eleven. They were very proud. They wanted to show their mettle. They wanted to abolish slavery. They all wanted to do their best."

It's believed that Price, however, was white. A farmer from Saratoga, he enlisted on April 9, 1863, and was mustered out nearly two and a half years later on August 20, 1865.

"Many other white soldiers joined black regiments," said Lance Ingmire, a local Civil War historian. "He is listed as living in Wilton, a farmer, in the 1890 veterans pension list. In those days, your race was listed in all census data. There is just no documentation that he was black. He would have enlisted and been told what unit to fight with. There really wasn't a choice."

Price's grave is found right inside the cemetery gate, off Lincoln Avenue, one of several circling the American flag.

Other Civil War soldiers buried in this area include Henry Skidmore and Horace H. Henry, who fought with the Harris Light Cavalry, the name given to the Second New York Light Cavalry Regiment, named after U.S. senator Ira Harris of Albany, who filled William Seward's seat after Seward became President Lincoln's secretary of state.

Harris's daughter, Clara, and her fiancé, Major Henry Reed Rathbone, were both in the balcony with President and Mrs. Lincoln the night John Wilkes Booth assassinated Lincoln in Ford's Theatre. After shooting the president, Booth slashed Rathbone's arm to the bone before dramatically leaping out of the balcony, breaking his leg and making a getaway.

Two other men—Montezulia Simmons and Lewis LaRose—served with the 118th New York Infantry, known as the Adirondack Regiment, which saw considerable action during the war.

The cemetery's Civil War monument is predominantly surrounded by soldiers of the 77th New York Volunteer Infantry Regiment, better known as the Bemis Heights Regiment, named for the Battles of Saratoga from the Revolutionary War. It was one of two regiments from Saratoga County; the 115th was the other. The 77th was composed mainly of men from in and around Saratoga Springs. One of its members buried in Greenridge is Lieutenant William J. Tabor, who was killed at the Battle of Cedar Creek, Virginia, on October 19, 1864.

The 115th enlisted more from outlying towns to the north and west.

In January 1863, President Lincoln instituted the first federal draft in history and called for an additional 300,000 men to fill ranks decimated by death, disease and desertion. Regiments were supposed to be 1,000-men strong. By 1863, however, most were down to about 300. If not for the draft and more volunteers, the North wouldn't have prevailed at Gettysburg in the first three days of July 1863, one of the war's main turning points.

"New York supplied more Northern troops than any other state, because we had a larger population, and suffered the second-most casualties after Pennsylvania," Bodnar said.

The Seventy-seventh served for the war's duration from 1861 to 1865, taking part in all the campaigns of the Army of the Potomac. It also fought at the Battle of Fort Stevens in defense of Washington, D.C., and served under General Sherman in the Shenandoah Valley.

Among those who served with the 115th was Lieutenant Colonel George Sherman Batcheller, a Harvard-trained lawyer who, at age twenty-one, became New York's youngest state legislator before joining the Union army at twenty-six. During the war, he became a judge advocate of military law, overseeing court-martials and military issues for the Department of the South.

Batcheller was born in 1837 in the hamlet of Batchellerville, town of Edinburgh, in western Saratoga County. At that time, there was no Great Sacandaga Lake. In 1873, eight years after the Civil War, Batcheller built an extravagant three-story, eleven-bedroom Saratoga Springs home on Circular Street known as Batcheller Mansion.

One of his guests was President Ulysses S. Grant, who named him judge and American representative in the Court of First Instance in Cairo, Egypt, where the Batchellers lived for ten years. Grant visited Saratoga Springs multiple times, and his love for the area enticed him to take up residence at Mount McGregor, where he finished his memoirs hours before his death on July 23, 1865.

In 1890, after returning to Saratoga Springs, the Batchellers entertained the lord chief justice of England and the American Bar Association at their mansion.

Batcheller and his wife, Catherine, are buried in an Egyptian-style mausoleum at Greenridge Cemetery.

Others, with simpler graves, include the likes of Captain Seth W. Deyoe (1836–1909), who enlisted in 1862 and was shot in the eye at Spotsylvania Courthouse during General Grant's Overland Campaign. Discharged, he came home, got married, ran a farm in the town of Saratoga and eventually became deputy sheriff in Saratoga Springs.

An epitaph on the Greenridge Civil War monument sums up what local soldiers fought and died for: "Not for themselves, but for their country."

THE BLACKWOOD BROTHERS, HADLEY

Published May 25, 2009

Two brothers, one of whom died in a Confederate prison camp, were part of one of the most bizarre tales in Civil War history.

George and William Blackwood, of Hadley Hill, were among the hundreds of Saratoga County residents who fought in the War Between the States and were typical of the men who came from small towns and rural farm country.

They joined the Union army at Camp Mohawk in Fonda in September 1862 and were sent directly to Harper's Ferry to engage Robert E. Lee's Army of Northern Virginia, the first in a series of battles known as Lee's Maryland Campaign.

"Lee was making a concerted effort to bring the battles of the Civil War to the North," said Lance Ingmire, a town of Saratoga resident, avid Civil War historian and teacher at Empire State College. Ingmire is also a descendant of the Blackwoods—George Blackwood was his great-great-grandfather. Fourteen of his ancestors fought for the Union army from Saratoga and Albany Counties.

When the 115th New York Regiment got to Harper's Ferry, however, the Union commander in charge, Colonel Dixon Miles, capitulated, thinking that Lee's army had superior forces. All twelve thousand Union soldiers, including the Blackwoods, were taken prisoner. At the time, both Union and Confederate armies adhered to a strict code of honor in which captured soldiers agreed not to take up arms against their captors until exchanged. By today's standards, the policy seems unbelievable; at the time, it was taken seriously and enforced.

The two armies also had a policy of exchanging prisoners in equal numbers because neither side wanted to commit men and resources to holding the other's captured soldiers. At that point, however, the two armies couldn't make an equal exchange because the North had captured more soldiers than the South. So, adhering to a seemingly ridiculous code of honor, the 115th New York was sent to Camp Douglas in Chicago, where Northern soldiers were held under guard by their own Union army along with Rebel prisoners of war.

The Blackwoods, who signed up to fight, wanted no part of a prison camp and apparently skedaddled home to northern Saratoga County.

"They didn't live up to their enlistment," Ingmire said. "Technically, they went AWOL, which was known as desertion during the Civil War."

In January 1863, President Lincoln granted amnesty to any soldier who had taken unauthorized leave. Whether for that reason or because the authorities simply caught up with them, the two brothers rejoined their regiment. In the meantime, a prisoner exchange had taken place, and the 115th New York was sent to Beaufort, South Carolina. When they arrived, the men discovered that the entire regiment had been brought up on arson charges. While they were preparing to leave Camp Douglas, some barracks had caught fire. The Northern soldiers were suspected of starting the blaze.

"Then they became prisoners again of their own army," said Ingmire.

It turned out that the fire was accidental, as some heating stoves had been turned over to remove ashes. Some were hot and had started the blaze. So, after several months, the 115th Regiment was exonerated, and the Blackwoods went back to the business of fighting a war.

"Because they were in the South, they were used in some of the South's many battles," Ingmire said.

One of the more famous was at Olustee, Florida—about midway between Jacksonville and Tallahassee—on February 20, 1864, the largest Civil War battle in Florida. The Union's objectives were to occupy Jacksonville in order to disrupt transportation links and deprive the Confederacy of food supplies from central Florida; capture cotton, turpentine and timber; gain black recruits for the Union army; and induce Unionists in east Florida to organize a loyal state government.

After securing Jacksonville, Union forces began moving westward. Confederates set up a defensive position at Olustee with Ocean Pond on one side, a nearly impassable swamp on the other and a narrow passageway in between. By nightfall, the Union had retreated, having suffered 1,861 casualties—William Blackwood among them—twice that of the Confederates.

For the number of soldiers involved, it was one of the war's bloodiest battles.

"William was shot and left in the field during the retreat," Ingmire said. "He was captured by Confederates and taken to Andersonville. He died there of his wounds. I've been down there to see his grave."

Andersonville, in Georgia, was one of the South's most notorious prison camps, where thousands of Northern soldiers died of disease, starvation and untreated battle wounds.

The Union occupied Jacksonville for the rest of the war, fighting Rebels along the coast, but it never tried to move into west Florida again.

George Blackwood stayed with his unit and later fought at Cold Harbor, Virginia, in June 1864, when he was wounded in the leg and festered in the field for three days.

"The only thing that saved his life were maggots," Ingmire said. "They ate the tissue and killed the infection."

The 115th also took part in the Siege of Petersburg and was in the vicinity of Appomattox when Lee surrendered to Grant on April 9, 1865. George Blackwood came back home to work the family farm and died in 1910. He's buried in Luzerne.

The regiment held reunions for decades to come, thanks largely to the efforts of Sergeant Nicholas DeGraff of Amsterdam, who kept an active mailing list and did a great deal of work on behalf of his fellow veterans. In 1925, he closed the 115th's 63rd anniversary gathering with a statement that read, in part:

Rejoicing with comrades of our other wars in the stability of our government and the happiness of our people, under the favor and blessing of Almighty God, we rest from the great work that we did in reclaiming our brothers of the southland from their error of secession and restoring the flag to its sovereign place at the head of a united people, which grows in magnitude and importance as the years multiply.

For further reading, see The 115th New York in the Civil War: A Regimental History *by Mark Silo.*

GRANT'S COTTAGE, WILTON

Published July 25, 2000

This week 115 years ago, the entire world mourned the death of President Ulysses S. Grant, who passed away at Mount McGregor on July 23, 1885.

The Civil War hero had completed his memoirs just three days before succumbing to a lengthy and excruciating battle with throat cancer.

This weekend, hundreds of visitors, including a group of Union reenactment soldiers, turned out to honor Grant's memory at the mountaintop cottage where he spent the last five weeks of his life.

"These kind of events help me get a sense of history," said Carl Zeh of Greenfield. "When I'm meeting these people and they're dressed

Grant's Cottage, Wilton, where President Ulysses S. Grant died on July 23, 1885, shortly after finishing his memoirs.

in actual uniforms with artifacts…it puts this millennium we're in and country in perspective."

The president lived at the cottage from June 16 to July 23, 1885, often working through the night to finish his memoirs with the encouragement of close friend Mark Twain, whose publishing company paid Grant $500,000 for the work. Despite being a military hero, Grant was penniless at his death because of bad business decisions. His memoirs not only served history but also were a dying man's last struggle to provide for his family.

What became known as Grant's Cottage was built in the 1870s by Duncan McGregor as a small boardinghouse. It originally occupied a spot at the mountain's very summit but was moved to its present position to make way for the Balmoral Hotel, owned by Joseph W. Drexel, which opened in 1884.

Drexel owned the cottage when Grant came there to escape the summertime heat of New York City. He also built a narrow-gauge railroad that ran from Saratoga Springs to his mountaintop hotel, a forty-five-minute trip.

"Originally, it was intended to go all the way to Lake George," said tour guide Dolores Corrigan. "However, this is as far as it ever got."

She described Grant as more than a Civil War hero in the North, but as someone regaled by heads of state in foreign nations as well. By bringing the war to a swift conclusion after being named commander, he restored international trade to European countries that needed many of the goods and products America had to offer.

"Northern England's fabric mills needed cotton," Corrigan said. "He took over at a point where the war had to be ended. That's why he was chosen. When Lincoln chose Grant, the rest of the world considered him a hero."

"Grant was the ultimate general, a quintessential general," she continued. "If you wrote a job description for general, it would be Grant. He was probably the worst businessman in political history. He left the army one time, ruined a few businesses and went back into the army. But he was a general."

This weekend's Civil War reenactment soldiers spent time discussing camp life and warfare with visitors and tented overnight on the grounds of Wilton Heritage Museum at the foot of Mount McGregor. Their presence was fitting because numerous Civil War veterans had in fact paid tribute to Grant by traveling to Mount McGregor during his final days and parading before him while he rested on the porch of Grant's Cottage.

The president's death was hastened by an unfortunate set of circumstances. He would make regular trips in a small wagon to the mountain's overlook to enjoy sweeping panoramic views of the Upper Hudson Valley and Vermont's Taconic Range and Green Mountains.

One day, however, the train dropped coal in the wagon's path, meaning Grant had to walk the remaining few hundred yards back to the cottage. Already weakened by cancer, the feat proved more than he could handle, and he passed away shortly after 8:00 a.m. one day later.

His body lay in state at Mount McGregor for ten days before it was taken to New York City, where throngs turned out to the largest funeral procession the city had ever seen. Grant had wanted to be buried at Arlington National Cemetery or West Point, but rules forbid women being buried at either place, so Grant opted for a site in New York City because he wanted his wife's final resting spot at his side.

Many people think of Grant's drinking habits whenever his name is mentioned. While acknowledging that this was a weakness, Corrigan said it wasn't as pronounced as some historians claim, and she told a story to put things in perspective.

Frustrated by other generals' lack of resolve, Lincoln scanned a list of leaders to assume command of Union forces at a critical point during the war. When Grant's name was mentioned, someone protested, "Mr. President, he's a heavy drinker!"

To which Lincoln replied, "Find out what brand of whiskey he likes, and make sure all my generals get some."

GRANT FREQUENTED SARATOGA SPRINGS

Published September 17, 2009

President Ulysses S. Grant and his wife, Julia, were a nineteenth-century version of Romeo and Juliet, two people totally devoted to each other and whose devotion carried them through great personal difficulty and some of the most trying times in American history.

In the 1870s, they frequented Saratoga Springs quite regularly because of the Civil War hero's great love for horses. They were also guests of the Spa City's social elite, such as the Vanderbilts and Batchellers, whose Circular Street mansion had to be finished ahead of schedule to host a reception for Grant in 1874.

This weekend, the first couple, portrayed by Larry and Connie Clowers, will be among the star attractions at a Civil War encampment at Congress

Park, featuring camp life, military demonstrations and visits by President Lincoln and Confederate general Robert E. Lee.

"This is so important," Clowers (Grant) said. "It keeps our history alive. Union soldiers who came from here grew up in the cradle of American history. They were born in the 1820s and '30s and heard their grandfathers tell stories about Saratoga and Bemis Heights in the Revolution. This is what we want to instill in young people—passion for our country."

Clowers has been portraying Grant for more than twenty years and lives in Gettysburg, Pennsylvania.

From abject poverty, Grant rose to fame in just a matter of years as commander of

President Ulysses S. and Julia Grant visited Saratoga Springs many times, as told by reenactors Larry and Connie Clowers of Gettysburg, Pennsylvania.

Union forces during the War Between the States. It is a lesson in overcoming adversity that the Clowers will share with Maple Avenue Middle School students throughout the day on Friday.

"We dispel a lot of the myths about Grant—that he was a drunk and butcher," Larry Clowers said. "He wasn't perfect. No one is a saint, but he was a man who had problems and overcame them. He was always able to focus on what the real issue was. We share this message with young people all the time."

Clowers, just as Grant might have, also displays a genuine sense of humor.

Walking into Adirondack Trust Co., he turned quite a few heads.

"I think I made a five dollar deposit here in 1873," he said. "It's time to collect the interest."

Someone suggested that Adirondack Trust, which is sponsoring this week's encampment, should give away fifty-dollar bills—bearing Grant's likeness—in honor of the president's visit.

"That's the bank down the street," bank CEO, chairman and president Charles Wait joked.

When he was told that President Barack Obama might visit Saratoga County next week, Grant (Clowers) said, "I outrank him. I was the eighteenth president. I have seniority."

The real Grant was thoroughly amazed by the horseflesh he found at Saratoga Race Course, which opened in 1863, the same year he led the Union to victory at Vicksburg, a turning point of the Civil War.

Raised in rural Ohio, he was the most accomplished horseman in his class at West Point. However, he'd always admired the animals for the work they could perform, essential to everyday life in the 1800s.

Saratoga was the first place he saw high-quality thoroughbreds raised solely for racing.

During a two-and-a-half-year world tour, from 1877 to 1879, he brought home two Arabians named Leopard and Linden Tree, a gift from the Ottoman Empire's sultan.

One time, Grant was overheard to say, "My passion and love are horses and my children."

To which Julia responded, "I'd like a word with you."

In reality, she held first place in his heart. Even on his deathbed at Mount McGregor in Wilton, Grant struggled to complete his memoirs so that his wife and family would have an income to live on after his passing.

"He would never see a penny for this," Clowers said. "Everything he did was for his family."

INDIAN WARS

SERGEANT JAMES BUTLER: CUSTER'S LAST STAND

Published November 15, 2009

Sergeant James Butler died in the most famous battle ever fought on American soil west of the Mississippi River. On June 25, 1876, the Ballston native was among the 263 soldiers killed at the Battle of Little Bighorn, under the command of Lieutenant Colonel George Custer.

A monument to Butler's memory stands at St. Mary's Cemetery in Ballston Spa, although he's buried at Custer National Cemetery, near the battlefield where he fell.

"Sergeant Butler was a soldier of many years' experience and known courage," General Edward S. Godfrey wrote in a report following the battle. "The indications were that he had sold his life dearly, for near and under him were found many cartridge shells. I believe he had been selected as a courier to communicate with [Major] Reno."

Butler, age thirty-four, of Company L, died attempting to get through the fighting to inform Major Reno that Custer wasn't faring well. While the five companies under Custer were annihilated, contrary to popular belief, not all federal troops were killed that day. Another 398 survived, along with 38 of 40 Native American scouts, and returned to Fort Abraham Lincoln near Bismarck, North Dakota, where Custer's ill-fated expedition had begun several weeks earlier.

Custer had been in command of the fort for two and a half years, since November 1873. The army's objective was to escort Northern Pacific Railroad workers as they moved west, and President Ulysses S. Grant had

A riderless horse stands at a stone marking the grave of Sergeant James Butler, who died in Custer's Last Stand at Little Bighorn, Montana.

issued an ultimatum that Native Americans be returned to their reservations by January 31, 1876. The Dakota Territory was under the command of General Terry at Fort Snelling in Minneapolis, and Terry told Custer to get the job done.

By early June, Custer's Seventh Cavalry was trailing the six bands of Lakota Sioux—led by Chief Sitting Bull and Crazy Horse—that had defied government orders and were headed north to Canada. The Native Americans, including some Cheyennes and a few Arapahos, were congregated in a large summer village numbering in the thousands, banded together for protection.

Custer was supposed to be joined by two other outfits, the Third Cavalry under General George Crook at Fort Federman, Wyoming, and a cavalry-infantry based at Fort Ellis, Montana, led by Colonel John Gibbons. On June 17, however, the Lakotas defeated Crook at the Battle of the Rosebud. Gibbons, meanwhile, was late in arriving.

On June 24, Crow scouts told Custer that the Sioux trail had veered off west toward Bighorn.

Instead of waiting, Custer ordered his men to break camp and move out on a thirteen- to fourteen-mile "Moonlight March," reaching his destination before dawn the next day. Before he could attack, however, a Native American party discovered his position, leaving the yellow-haired colonel with a difficult decision: move in or wait.

"He knew that if he waited, the Indians would scatter," said Al Johnson, historian at Fort Abraham Lincoln. "He took it upon himself to pursue them in an early morning action, but a lot of things went wrong. There was a lot of confusion."

On one hand, Custer was simply following orders. On the other, the Native Americans had an incredible advantage in numbers, and Custer's ego might have superseded good judgment.

"He was told he was badly outnumbered by his scouts," Johnson said. "He believed he could beat insurmountable odds."

"He want[ed] to go down there and get the victory," said Ken Woody, Little Bighorn Battlefield National Monument chief of interpretation. "He didn't care what the odds were. He was going to make it work."

"Custer's strategy will always be second-guessed, but he didn't have much choice," said Marvin Dawes, a National Park Service ranger at the historic site.

"At sunrise, the Native Americans knew Custer was there," Dawes continued. "So what do you do in that situation? You'd be surprised. A lot of people, if they were in his boots, would have made the same movement. When you're pursuing your enemy, you've got to keep moving. If they know you're there, you don't wait for reinforcements. You've got to move in."

The outcome was inevitable, and a stunned nation, celebrating its 100th birthday at the Philadelphia Exposition, couldn't believe the news as shocking reports slowly filtered back East.

A monument atop Last Stand Hill is dedicated to the soldiers, such as Butler, who died on the Montana plains that day. Markers in the field show where they fell. In many cases, two simple stones stand side by side in the tall grass because, in their final minutes, soldiers would fight in pairs—their backs together—to the end.

Many in the Seventh Cavalry were born in Europe and immigrated to the United States, only to die in a place that hadn't yet officially joined the Union. Butler first enlisted in the army on May 31, 1870, five years after the Civil War. He reenlisted on May 31, 1875, and was killed just over a year later. His body was buried where he fell and was rediscovered in 1903.

Unknown Grave

Butler's body was believed to have been removed from his original grave in Deep Coulee in 1903 by the War Department and reinterred in an unknown grave at Custer National Cemetery, a part of Little Bighorn Battlefield National Monument, where the battle occurred.

An eleven-foot obelisk memorial erected on Last Stand Hill is inscribed with the names of all battle casualties on all four sides, including that of Butler.

His reinterment is thought to have been on June 25, 1903, when former blacksmith Henry Meckling, of Company H, Seventh Cavalry, and a Medal of Honor recipient at Little Bighorn, visited the battlefield and identified several grave sites, including one between the Custer Battlefield and the Reno-Benteen Battlefield.

Custer isn't buried at the national cemetery that bears name. His body was brought back and buried at the United States Military Academy at West Point.

WORLD WAR I

THE GURTLER BROTHERS: CASUALTIES OF WAR

Published July 2, 2009

The Spa City knows how to celebrate the Stars and Stripes as well as any place in America. One of the grandest displays in its history took place when local doughboys returned home from fighting overseas in World War I.

A multitude of red, white and blue flags and bunting greeted soldiers as they arrived by train at the old Delaware & Hudson depot on Railroad Place, with Division Street, Broadway and Lake Avenue equally adorned. A large banner read, "Welcome Home Company L: Saratoga's Own."

Saratoga Springs alone lost twenty-six young men, while dozens of others from throughout Saratoga County paid the supreme sacrifice in the Great War that was supposed to end all wars.

"The casualties were astronomical in World War I compared to today, even World War II," said James M. Coyne, adjutant of Gurtler Brothers VFW Post No. 420. "A lot of casualties were near the end of the war. Most were buried in France. It was the most expedient way. You have to think of those massive numbers."

One cemetery in France is the final resting place of 25,000 Americans. In the army alone, New York State lost 12,356 soldiers (62 from Saratoga County), and disease claimed almost as many (4,566) as those killed in action (5,173).

Corporal William and Private George Gurtler Jr., for whom the Saratoga Springs VFW Post is named, are among the tens of thousands

Veterans Jim Coyne (left) and Ed Freiberger display memorabilia related to the Gurtler brothers, who fought and died in World War I. Gurtler Brothers VFW Post in Saratoga Springs is named after them.

of American World War I heroes buried in France. "The two brothers, whose wish it had been to fight together in the same company, were killed by the same shell in the assault on San Souplet," *The Saratogian* reported. "Both died instantly. The last word from the two came in letters written on the same day and received by Mr. and Mrs. George Gurtler Sr. (31 Jumel Place) at the same time."

The Gurtlers died on October 20, 1918, less than a month before the war's end. A letter dated November 1 from their acting commanding officer, Lieutenant Herbert S. Conant, told of their valor. "Your sons were held in the highest favor by all in the company, William being a candidate for the next Officers Training School," he told their parents. "No harder workers in the company, they were noble, efficient soldiers and were the bravest of the brave."

When the brothers first enlisted, Company L was a National Guard unit, and the United States hadn't yet entered the war. One of their first duties was the Mexican Border Conflict in 1916. In March, General John "Black Jack" Pershing led four thousand U.S. troops to quell raids led by Pancho Villa into the United States. Increasing tension led to the threat of war, and in June,

President Woodrow Wilson called out the National Guard to help deal with the problem. The situation was quickly settled without major hostilities.

On April 6, 1917, however, the Gurtlers had a different fate when the United States declared war on Germany.

"We did not have a large standing army, so the government would federalize these units and send them wherever they needed them," Coyne said.

War in Europe

Company L arrived in Brest, France, on May 30, 1918, just in time for some of the war's bloodiest, most intense fighting. Heavy belts of barbed wire, horrific shelling and machine-gun fire typified trench warfare of the day. From September 27 to 29, Company L's soldiers helped break through the famed German Hindenburg Line, a vast defense system in northeast France.

"In World War I, the Allies never got into Germany," Coyne said. "Most of the fighting was in France and Belgium. The Allies won, but the Germans never surrendered. It was an armistice. They stopped fighting. They ran out of manpower and supplies."

Sergeant Melville Cady—Company G, Twenty-eighth Infantry, First Division, U.S. Regulars—was one of two Greenfield Center native sons who died in the war. On July 14, 1918, he suffered shrapnel wounds in the back and right leg during the Battle of Soissons but returned to action in late August. In October, the twenty-two-year-old was killed in action and later buried with twenty-five thousand other Americans in the Argonne, about twenty miles north of Verdun.

Corporal Rowland Waterbury of Saratoga Springs was somewhat unique among war casualties; his body was brought home and buried at Greenridge Cemetery. He was the only son of Louise and W.R. Waterbury, a prominent Spa City businessman, proprietor of Waterbury's Clothing Store on Broadway, school board president during the 1880s and '90s and a bank director.

Just shy of graduation from Williams College, Rowland Waterbury enlisted in the Seventy-seventh Regulars of New York City and went to France. "He was wounded in the big push that broke the Hindenburg Line on the morning of Sept. 29, 1918, and died in France on Oct. 26," *The Saratogian* reported.

The story of Coyne's uncle James E. Coyne, of Rensselaer, was one of the war's most poignant. A U.S. Marine Corps private, he was wounded at Belleau Wood. On November 11, 1918, the world celebrated the end of hostilities. Three days later, Coyne's family was notified that his wounds had proved fatal. Like Waterbury, however, his body was brought home.

"He's one of the few," James M. Coyne said.

The United States had fought European foes before—in the Revolution, the War of 1812, the Mexican War and the Spanish-American War—but World War I was the first time America had been brought onto the world stage as an ally. "We probably tipped the scales in favor of the Allies when we entered the war," Coyne said. "It gave them unlimited manpower."

Those who made it back got a much-deserved hero's welcome, just like their sons would a quarter century later at the conclusion of World War II. "That pretty much ended after World War II," Coyne said. "Korean vets came home and were ignored. We [Vietnam vets] came home and were abused. Since Desert Storm, the pendulum's swung back. I'm pleased that they're not doing what they did to us."

Veterans Fight for Bonus

Thousands of World War I veterans were victims of one of the ugliest incidents in U.S. history. In 1924, Congress voted to give them a bonus for wartime duty—$1.25 per day overseas, $1.00 per day in the States. However, the provision wouldn't take effect until 1945. By 1932, the nation was in the depths of the Great Depression, and thousands of veterans were unemployed and wanted their money right away.

In May 1932, a fifteen-thousand-man Bonus Army of veterans descended on the nation's capital, living in tents and shacks and waiting for payment.

On June 17, more than ten thousand veterans crowded the Capitol grounds as the Senate voted on a bill that the House had already passed that would have given veterans their money. To their disbelief, the measure failed, sixty-two to eighteen. The men began a month-long silent Death March in front of the Capitol to protest their fate.

On July 28, the U.S. attorney general ordered the evacuation of veterans from government property. Washington, D.C. police were met with resistance, shots were fired and two marchers were killed. President Hoover then directed the army to clear out the veterans. Late that same afternoon, veterans massed on Pennsylvania Avenue below the Capitol. A cavalry unit and infantry with fixed bayonets charged and hurled tear gas into the crowd.

Veterans fled across the Anacostia River to their main camp. Hoover ordered the army, under the command of General Douglas MacArthur, to stop, but MacArthur routed and torched the camp. Some families had been present, and two babies were killed. By morning, local hospitals were filled with casualties, most of them World War I veterans who had risked everything in defense of their country.

"Their promises weren't met," Coyne said.

One outcome of the Bonus Army's protest, however, was the eventual adoption of the GI Bill of Rights, passed in July 1944, which helped returning World War II veterans fit back into civilian life.

"The GI Bill might have been the greatest thing our government ever did," Coyne said. "You don't honor the war, you honor the warrior."

WORLD WAR II

DANTE ORSINI: AT FDR'S SIDE

Published December 7, 2007

A stunned, fearful and suddenly unsure nation hung on President Roosevelt's every word as he described December 7, 1941, as a date that would live in infamy.

Dan Orsini of South Glens Falls was there for FDR's monumental speech as a twenty-one-year-old U.S. Marine assigned to the Capitol and White House honor guard.

A few weeks later, on Christmas Eve, Orsini met Winston Churchill at Washington's official Christmas tree lighting, and while serving overseas, he was personally decorated by Chinese leader Chiang Kai-shek.

"I got to shake hands with both the president and Winston Churchill," said Orsini, now eighty-seven. "They relied on each other and they trusted each other. World War II was a war that had to be fought and had to be won. Everybody looked to Roosevelt to win this war. I had tremendous feeling for the man."

For a small-town kid who joined the service because there weren't many jobs available, his brush with world leaders provided a lifetime of memories.

"I was fortunate to have been at many places with the president," he said.

He still has the official White House invitation to FDR's third inauguration. He sat at the Inaugural Ball with entertainer Mickey Rooney and twice rode aboard the president's train to the "Little White House" in Warm Springs, Georgia. He was also there when Roosevelt dedicated the Jefferson Memorial

Dante Orsini of South Glens Falls was a member of President Franklin D. Roosevelt's White House U.S. Marine Corps honor guard and later served in the Pacific.

on April 13, 1943. Later that year, Orsini was promoted to sergeant major, the highest enlisted rank, although he was still just twenty-three years old.

After going through officer's training school, he was commissioned a second lieutenant but shunned the rank because of the domestic duties involved. Instead, he went back to sergeant major in order to join his First Division marines in the Pacific.

"I was with people I wanted to be with," Orsini said. "I was ready to go over. That's what I wanted to do anyway, all along."

At Guam, during a clandestine operation to the island of Rota, he took charge when the patrol's leader was killed. A commendation letter from the commanding general says it all: "The success of the whole operation depended largely upon the instruction and advice offered by this man [Orsini]."

Assigned to a machine-gun unit, he took part in the invasion of Okinawa that cost fourteen thousand Americans their lives and would have gone to the Japanese mainland if President Truman hadn't authorized the atomic bombing of Hiroshima and Nagasaki.

"That's one of the greatest decisions any president ever made," Orsini said. "He saved millions of lives, especially Americans. It was a decision that had to be made."

From there, the marines went to China to help keep peace between government and communist forces. "We had skirmishes, and some of our guys got killed there," he said.

In Peking's Tiananmen Square, Chiang Kai-shek honored marines with the Order of the Cloud and Banner medal.

A South Glens Falls native, Orsini joined the service in early 1940, almost two full years before Pearl Harbor Day. He recalls that memorable Sunday with vivid clarity.

"It was one o'clock in the afternoon, and I was playing basketball at the U.S. Naval War College, in Washington," he said. "The announcement came over that Pearl Harbor had been bombed. What could we do then? We said, well let's finish the game. Then we'll find out what's going on."

Twenty-four hours later, the full gravity of the situation had finally sunk in. Standing at attention in dress blues, Orsini watched as President Roosevelt asked Congress for a declaration of war.

"It only lasted a half hour, but there must have been five thousand people there," he said.

> *We knew what he was going to say. We felt like we had to go to war. We had no choice. All of a sudden the U.S. changed. We could no longer be the peaceful country we wanted to be.*
>
> *That was a very exciting and very emotional speech. He spoke from the heart and was very, very upset that the United States had been attacked. Roosevelt had to gear the country up to fight the war, and that's what he did. He led it.*

In tribute to the nation's sacrifice, the 1941 Christmas tree lighting was the last on the White House grounds for the duration of the war. Roosevelt and Churchill used the occasion, via radio, to assure worldwide listeners that the resolve of freedom-loving peoples everywhere would win the war.

"Our strongest weapon in this war is that conviction of the dignity and brotherhood of man which Christmas Day signifies—more than any other day or any other symbol," Roosevelt said. "Against enemies who preach the principles of hate and practice them, we set our faith in human love and in God's care for us and all men everywhere."

SNOWDON SMITH: PEARL HARBOR PURPLE HEART

Published December 5, 2004

Snowdon Smith has never been back to Pearl Harbor. Once was enough.

An Army Air Corps pilot, he arrived there early on Friday, December 5, 1941, en route to a reconnaissance mission over Japan, seeking intelligence

Snowdon Smith was shot and lost his leg during the Japanese attack on Pearl Harbor on December 7, 1941.

Elizabeth Smith looks at a newspaper headline telling about the Japanese attack on Pearl Harbor, where her husband, Snowdon, was wounded.

about the Japanese fleet. Two days later, he was up bright and early, preparing for the day's activity.

"I heard a lot of noise," he said. "Bang, bang, bang. I couldn't see it from where I was. I happened to be glancing at one end of the airfield, and a loose formation of planes was flying along. Then the first bomb dropped. It made a helluva noise."

"Geez, somebody's going to get court-martialed for that," Smith thought to himself.

But reality quickly hit home, quite literally.

"I rubbed my hand over my head only to see and feel fresh blood," he said. "I looked next to me and saw my companions lying dead with their brains literally hanging out. I thought they were my brains, so I thought I was dying for sure."

He looked down to find his lower leg hanging on by an inch of skin. It had to be removed, and because of infections, he underwent five amputations during the next two years, the last well above his knee.

Smith was one of World War II's first American wounded.

"I probably got hit in the first three or four minutes of the attack. My part in the war was pretty much over right then and there," he said. "They wanted to immobilize our aircraft. They were strafing and dropping bombs on our hangars. I was standing right outside one of the hangars."

"I was removed, fortunately, between the first and second attacks," Smith continued. "I think I was in the back of a truck."

Today, at eighty-eight, Smith lives at Wesley Health Care Center and suffers from Alzheimer's disease. Thanks to his foresight, his vivid memories of Pearl Harbor were preserved during a taped interview, made three years ago.

"I remember waking up and saw that it was gone," Smith said of his leg. "What could I do? It was pretty silly to lie there and think I'd like to do this and do that. I wasn't going to be able to."

After the attack, he started having nightmares.

"I would be running away from this Japanese cartoon character flying a plane. I just kept running until I woke up. I would see these dead bodies everywhere," he said.

Once his leg was sufficiently healed, Smith fought to stay active in the service.

"He wrote all kinds of letters, and he finally did make it again as an operations officer, and he went to Tarawa," said his daughter, Brooke Smith, of Saratoga Springs. "He was there till the end of the war."

"I was sorry that I couldn't keep up with the flying end of it," he said.

A love for aviation is what drew him into the service in the first place. A Syracuse native, he joined the Army Air Corps in February 1940, less than a year after graduating from Syracuse University.

"That was the best way in those days of learning how to fly," Smith said.

Following basic training at Tuscaloosa, Alabama, he was assigned to a heavy reconnaissance squadron in Salt Lake City and flew a B-17. Smith and his wife, Elizabeth, his childhood sweetheart, were married there on October 27, 1941. She went out to meet him because there was no way he could get home for a wedding.

During their short-lived honeymoon, Smith got orders to report for a highly classified operation.

"We didn't know what the mission was," he said. "It was all hush-hush and very secret at the time."

U.S. intelligence didn't have the benefit of today's high-tech spy satellites, and there was uncertainty about the Japanese fleet's location. His job was to fly low over a sensitive part of Japan, where the fleet might be harbored, and take surveillance photographs.

As fate would have it, he never got there. Smith had achieved the rank of captain by the time the war ended and was awarded a Purple Heart because of his injuries.

In the early 1950s, he was among a group of disabled veterans who paid President Truman a personal visit. The encounter took place in the Oval Office.

"They corralled a bunch of us to show the president what we were doing. One of these men had both arms gone. He had artificial arms strapped on him. He took them off over his head, and these arms plopped down on the president's desk. He almost fell off his chair," Smith said with a laugh.

Several soldiers, like Smith, had lost a leg, and when their turn came, they showed off their prosthetics while standing proudly before the commander in chief in nothing but their underwear.

Smith was still a young man, having experienced more than his fair share of heartbreak. His recollection of the moment perhaps best explains why he went on to lead such a productive life after suffering so much.

"He was all right," Smith said of Truman. "But I remember looking at him and thinking: 'The problems this poor man has.'"

FRED MICHALOFSKY: PEARL HARBOR SURVIVOR

Published Sunday December 7, 2003

Just try following Frances Michalofsky someday. That's what this reporter did after noticing the words "Pearl Harbor Survivor" on her license plate.

Heading south toward Saratoga Springs, she turned off Route 9 onto Maple Avenue, cut across North Broadway, went behind Wesley Health Care Center, down Seward Avenue, through an apartment complex and finally entered Saratoga Hospital's parking lot, where I caught up with her.

Fortunately, she has a sense of humor.

"I kept wondering who that was," said Frances, who lives in Wilton.

"Who's the Pearl Harbor survivor?" I asked after identifying myself.

"It was my late husband," she replied.

Fred Michalofsky spent more than three years in the army as a private in the 713th Tank Battalion that served in the Pacific Theatre of Operations. One of his first and most unforgettable experiences was the Japanese attack on Pearl Harbor on December 7, 1941.

Michalofsky drove a New York City taxi for most of his adult life. It wasn't until he retired to Saratoga County in 1990 that he had the designation "Pearl Harbor Survivor" put on his car's license plates.

"He had those plates for about nine years," said his daughter, Helene.

Fred Michalofsky passed away three years ago.

His wife, Frances, doesn't need reminding that he was someone special. The license plates send a message to others.

"I went to Motor Vehicles after Fred passed away, and they said, 'You keep that plate,'" she said.

The other day, she came out of a doctor's office and found a note attached to her windshield: "Thank you very much for serving your country."

While traveling down the Northway recently, a car pulled up alongside her, and its passengers gave Frances Michalofsky a thumbs-up, a salute that filled her with overwhelming pride.

"Fred said he never gave anyone trouble in the service," she said. "He was a good soldier. He was very well liked. My husband was very quiet."

She has no photo albums of his wartime days, only a picture or two of him in uniform. Pearl Harbor anniversaries came and went, and for nearly sixty years he shared few details about his experiences that fateful Sunday morning.

"I guess he didn't want to remember too much," Michalofsky said. "But he liked everything about the service. If there was anything about it on television or at the movies, he was right there."

After marrying, the couple lived in Elizabeth, New Jersey, for many years. They had met at a dance in New York.

"I was standing there waiting for someone to ask me to dance; then, Fred came along," Michalofsky said.

She said that Fred's only regret was that they didn't meet before he went in the army.

"He used to tell me, 'If I knew you then, you would have sent me some good food,'" she said with a laugh. "He told me the food was terrible."

Fred Michalofsky got the idea of having special license plates after noticing another Pearl Harbor survivor with them in Albany.

"He said, 'That's a memory of when I was in Pearl Harbor,'" Frances said. "After that, everybody started stopping us and talking to me and Fred. It's so nice when people talk to me—very, very nice. I just wish he was here yet. It's not the same since my husband's gone. It's quiet."

A Son Remembers

Jeff Michalofsky didn't fully appreciate his father's service to his country until later on in life. When the time comes, he'll make sure that his own five-year-old son, Robbie, has a full understanding of what Pearl Harbor was all about.

"Maybe we might even make a trip to Hawaii one day and see the memorial," Michalofsky said. "It would be very meaningful."

Pearl Harbor Day evokes a variety of emotions for him. One is sorrow for his father's passing three years ago. Another, more powerful, is pride about his military record.

"He was proud to be a veteran," Michalofsky said. "Veterans Day was a big day to him. He seemed very happy to have been a soldier."

Jeff said that his father volunteered for military service prior to Pearl Harbor.

"I know a couple of his brothers were upset because they weren't physically able to," he said.

His father served with a tank outfit in the Pacific, seeing combat in places such as Saipan and Tinian.

"He reminisced about wartime quite a bit," Michalofsky said. "Early on, I never paid much attention. It probably wasn't until I was in my late teens that I could appreciate the stories more."

"It was such a significant time in history," he continued. "It does mean a lot to me at this time of year. It gives you an awareness and makes you thankful for all that soldiers do to defend us."

Michalofsky said he wants to teach his son those lessons.

"That he should be proud of our army and defense system, that it's important," he said. "As big as the world is, you need a defense system to keep us free."

FRANK COPELAND: SAW THE JAPANESE ATTACK

Published December 3, 2006

Frank Copeland spent five years in the service. Two hours of it changed his life and world history forever.

Copeland, then eighteen, was sound asleep at Schofield Barracks on the Sunday morning of December 7, 1941, when the first wave of Japanese bombers flew overhead en route to Pearl Harbor, about eight miles away.

"On the other side of the road from our mess hall, we had this water storage tank," he said. "I guess the Japs thought that was a fuel tank of some sort, so they dropped a bomb on it. Then they started strafing us. Everything was going up in flames. It was about ten minutes I'd say before we realized a war was going on."

An army private, Copeland had enlisted in August 1940, more than a full year beforehand. Starting out at Fort Totten, Long Island, he was assigned to an antiaircraft unit and eventually made his way to Hawaii.

Frank Copeland shows a picture of himself taken during his army days. He was at Schofield Barracks on Oahu, Hawaii, when the Japanese attacked Pearl Harbor.

Japanese planes reached Oahu from the north, through Kolikole Pass, hitting one airfield after another on their way to the main target, Pearl Harbor, so that the U.S. flyers couldn't mount a response.

"Wheeler Field was right next to us," Copeland said. "The only thing separating us was a fence and a small pineapple field. All of a sudden, we heard all this racket outside, so we all got up and looked out there, with our shorts on. On Sundays, they used to practice dogfights. We'd see them all the time."

Then, however, the explosions started.

Running back inside, soldiers quickly dressed and scrambled to set up an antiaircraft battery. With the element of surprise on their side, the Japanese suffered few losses.

"You still had a few planes coming over," Copeland said. "We didn't get any, but just the other side of us a plane crashed there. I don't know if they got him with the .50-caliber machine guns or the antiaircraft. He was a Japanese lieutenant. They buried him right there."

In addition to Wheeler, a major fighter base, the first strike also targeted Hickam Army Airfield.

"They hit all these airfields all the way down to Pearl Harbor," Copeland said. "We could see the flashes and hear the bombs, even where we were at Schofield."

More than twenty-four hundred Americans were killed during the attack; the brunt of the devastation was borne by the U.S. Pacific Fleet at Pearl Harbor. Schofield wasn't immune to the carnage, though.

"One guy, the switchboard operator, they shot him right through the roof and got him sitting there," Copeland said.

After the initial shock, Copeland was sent to an ammunition center to get more supplies.

"We could look down to the harbor," he said. "All the ships were on fire."

The next day, his unit got orders to pack up and move to Kaneohe Bay, a naval marine base.

"That was all blown to heck, too," Copeland said. "That night we all hit the beaches. We stayed there all night long because we figured there'd be a land attack. But it never happened."

In the ensuing weeks, Copeland was randomly selected to join the Army Rangers.

"I got shanghaied into that," he said, chuckling. "They were supposed to be volunteers, but they took so many from each battery."

The training was about as tough as any the military had to offer—combat weapons, demolitions, jungle stream amphibious operations, platoon leadership, hand-to-hand techniques, knives, bayonets, grenades, jungle fighting techniques.

"They didn't do airborne, not then," he said. "But we did everything else the rangers do. Everything, you name it."

Copeland still has his ranger and combat training school graduation certificate. Unfortunately, he wasn't given his official black-and-gold ranger stripes until fifty years later, with help from the late U.S. representative Gerald B.H. Solomon.

Copeland proved himself so proficient that the army made him an instructor—one of the kindest hands fate could have dealt him. While the war moved into the Pacific, he stayed in Hawaii teaching young recruits how to become combat-ready.

"I was very, very lucky," he said, knocking on wood. "I'm dang glad that I was where I was. A lot of guys had it worse than I did."

Eventually, he did go overseas to the Gilbert Islands, where the marines had just taken Tarawa in some of the war's bloodiest, most brutal fighting.

"By that time the island was secured," he said. "When we got there, stuff was still floating on the beaches. There were dead Japs in the pillboxes. They didn't have them covered up. You could walk into any pillbox and they lay dead, rotting."

Copeland was still in the South Pacific on another momentous date—June 6, 1944—when the Allies invaded Normandy.

"We knew it was coming," he said. "They set up loudspeakers out in the battery area. It came over on D-Day."

Copeland had enlisted for a three-year hitch, but once the war started, he was in for the duration. Finally, in early 1945, his outfit was ordered back to Hawaii, a trip of four or five days.

"We had a destroyer escort in front of us," he said. "I don't know what happened, but they lost us. We had no contact. All of a sudden, all of the lights had to go out because we were being followed by a Jap submarine. We shut all the motors down and all the lights off. The next day the DE [escort] had to come back and find us and lead us back to Hawaii."

Sixty-five years have elapsed, and Copeland, now eighty-three, hasn't been back since, but he'd like to.

"I'd like to go back and see some of those places. I mean now I don't have to take orders," he said, laughing.

Copeland left the army the same way he went in, as a private.

"The highest I got was a corporal," he said. "I went to the mess hall one day for breakfast, and this sergeant we had, nobody liked him. We were eating, and somebody threw a pancake and hit me right in the face. It was on the table so I grabbed it, threw it back to hit him and hit the mess sergeant. From that time on, I was PFC [private first class]. I peeled a lot of potatoes. I got my share of KP and guard duty."

Like everyone else, he took the good with the bad and made the best of it.

A West Fort Ann native, Copeland lives in Queensbury with his son, Tim, and daughter-in-law, Susan (Hanshue), originally from Saratoga Springs. Her father, Jerome, was a longtime vice-president at Adirondack Trust Co.

In addition to raising a family, Copeland spent most of his working life in the construction business. At seventeen, he quit school to join the army.

"I just wanted to get away and do something different," he said. "That's all. It was an adventure."

Always looking for challenges, at an age when most people are already retired, he completed his high school education with a general equivalency degree.

"I wanted to see if I could do it or not," he said matter-of-factly.

On December 7, Copeland will reflect and heed the battle cry "Remember Pearl Harbor."

But do people really remember?

"I don't think they do now," he said. "They did at first. But then after a while it started to…It's done and over with."

But not for those who were there; not for those who lived through it.

"That's why his story is so important," Tim Copeland said. "It's history. Kids today need to know the importance of staying on guard."

JOHN FINN:
FIRST WORLD WAR II MEDAL OF HONOR RECIPIENT

Published July 23, 2009

John Finn survived the Japanese attack on Pearl Harbor and is just one day shy of becoming America's only one-hundred-year-old Medal of Honor recipient.

The California resident also served aboard the USS *Saratoga* aircraft carrier during a lengthy navy career and has visited the Spa City several times.

His secret for longevity? "Just keep breathing," he said, laughing. "That's the way I figure it."

He's not only America's oldest Medal of Honor recipient, but also, of the fifteen men who earned the award on December 7, 1941, he's the only one who remains. It's believed that he was World War II's first Medal of Honor recipient because the Naval Air Station at Kaneohe Bay, where he was stationed, was hit five minutes before Pearl Harbor.

Finn will celebrate his 100th birthday on Friday.

"Any airport has to have rigid rules and regulations about how the planes are supposed to come in," he said.

We heard planes flying around, but they weren't flying the station pattern. We figured out damn quick that they were attacking. The Japs were doing everything they could to destroy our military naval setup. They were shooting and dropping bombs and torpedoes. A lot of people, including myself, couldn't believe they were attacking us.

Completely disregarding his own safety, Finn manned a .50-caliber machine gun in an exposed area and kept fighting despite numerous wounds. He only left his post after being ordered to, and after getting medical attention, he returned to the squadron area and supervised the rearming of returning American warplanes. Doctors later identified twenty-one shrapnel marks in his chest and abdomen.

"To this day, I don't know if I shot anything down," Finn said.

Whether I shot any of the enemy down or not isn't as important as the fact that at least I fought back. I knew that no matter what, the men who were doing what those enemy pilots were doing, wasn't going to go unpunished, either by myself on that day or by our country in the future.

Finn joined the navy at age seventeen in July 1926.

"So many Pearl Harbor survivors were just young recruits. I had been in the navy fifteen years and had been a chief petty officer for six years. That's as high [as] an enlisted man can go without seeking a commission."

His first few years, however, were uneventful and didn't provide the kind of adventure he expected.

"I joined the navy to see the world," he said. "I just didn't get to sea. Nothing happens in a big hurry in the navy."

Finally, his chance came, and he joined the Asiatic fleet, went to China in the early 1930s and sailed up and down the coast all the way to the Philippines. During his career, Finn served with several aircraft squadrons on the USS *Houston*, USS *Saratoga*, USS *Lexington*, USS *Cincinnati* and USS *Hancock*. He was commissioned an ensign on October 6, 1942, promoted to lieutenant in May 1943 and retired from active duty two years after the war, in 1947.

Finn also holds a Purple Heart, a Navy Unit Commendation, a Good Conduct Medal with two bars, a Yangtze Service Medal, an American Defense Service Medal, an American Campaign Medal, an Asiatic-Pacific Campaign Medal and a World War II Victory Medal. However, the defining moment of his twenty-one-year career all comes down to fifteen bloody minutes on that fateful early Sunday morning.

In September 1998, Finn visited Saratoga Springs for a reunion of USS *Saratoga* crew members and dedication of its then–newly restored 930-pound bell. He was also here when the Spa City hosted a gathering of Medal of Honor recipients. On September 11, 2001, he was en route to Boston for another Medal of Honor reunion when terrorists struck the World Trade Center in New York and the Pentagon.

His plane put down in Albany, and he spent several days visiting friends in the Sacandaga area, including Thomas Hennessey, a shipmate from the USS *Hancock*.

"I don't get surprised very often," he said. "But that was a world-shaking event."

Finn and his late wife, Alice, were married sixty-six years. After the navy, he went into the repair business.

"I was always mechanically minded," he said. "I could do anything—cars, motorcycles, mostly household appliances. Anything but radios."

Today, he spends most of his time enjoying ranch life, east of San Diego. For his 100th birthday, there's one thing he's hoping for.

"More peace all over the world," he said. "That would be my most fervent wish."

EDWIN IVY: PRISONER OF WAR

Published January 1, 2009

For First Lieutenant Edwin Ivy, there were no Rose Parades, bowl games or family gatherings. He spent New Year's Day 1945 on a forced march from Stalag Luft III in Sagan, Poland, to a railhead at Spremberg, Germany, following more than seven months of internment as a prisoner of war.

Hollywood screen star and World War II veteran Clark Gable (left) presents American POW Edwin Ivy's Distinguished Flying Cross to Ivy's parents, Lillian Clark Ivy and Garland Ivy.

Ivy's camp was the same one depicted in the 1963 movie *The Great Escape*, starring Steve McQueen, which told the real-life story of a March 1944 Allied prison break.

An Army Air Corps navigator, Ivy's B-24 bomber was shot down over Vienna on May 29, 1944—one week before D-Day.

"We thought when D-Day came that we'd be out in short order," said Ivy, of Schuylerville. "It didn't happen that way. I spent eleven months in a POW camp. We were cold and hungry most of the time. It was subzero weather. I was down to 125 pounds from about 150."

Christmas brought a brief reprieve.

"One bowl of soup with a piece of meat about as big as your thumb," he said.

To the west, Germany had launched a major offensive—the Battle of the Bulge—designed to counter the Allied advance through Belgium, France and Luxembourg. Meanwhile, the Russians were closing in from the east.

"The Russians were about to over-run our camp," said the ninety-year-old Ivy, recalling events with vivid clarity. "So the Germans moved us to a railhead. We didn't know if we'd be treated as friends or not. This was war."

To reach their destination, POWs had to march four days through extreme weather.

"That's how I spent New Year's Day," he said. "The first night out I took my GI shoes off. They were sopping wet from melted snow, and they were frozen solid when I tried to put them back on in the morning. So I didn't take them off again till we got on the train at Spremberg. When I took them off, my toenails came off from frostbite."

From Spremberg, prisoners were shipped to Nuremberg, the site of a huge railroad-marshaling yard that came under constant attack from Allied bombers.

"So we had a ringside seat to the action for about a month," Ivy said. "The U.S. Air Corps was bombing every day, and the RAF [Royal Air Force] was bombing every night. Flak kept falling like hail. It was pretty exciting stuff."

Edwin Ivy, an Army Air Corps navigator, was shot down over Vienna on May 29, 1944, and spent months in a prisoner of war camp.

Stationed at Cerignola, in the "ankle of Italy's boot," Ivy had flown numerous missions, including Anzio and the infamous Raid on Ploesti, before being shot down while trying to bomb a German rail yard near Vienna.

"They had a lot of antiaircraft at Anzio," he said. "We came back with seventy-five holes in our plane, and the right tire was shot out. We had sort of a semi-crash landing. The flak was heavy, accurate and intense."

On its fateful flight over Vienna, Ivy's plane was knocked out of the sky shortly after delivering its payload.

"All of our crew got out alive," he said. "I parachuted and got to the edge of a forest, hiding behind a fallen tree. Things were pretty quiet for a while, so I stuck my head up."

Unfortunately, two German soldiers were standing nearby with a guard dog at their side. In their best English, they told Ivy, "For you, the war is over."

His worst ordeal, however, was just beginning. Following a week of interrogation, he was sent to Stalag Luft III, where Allied air force personnel were held.

"We were in rooms with about twelve people each," Ivy said.

We could walk around outside, but we didn't have the energy to do real exercise. We were starving most of the time, because the Germans kept half of our Red Cross parcels. The only thing we had enough of was coffee and tea. I learned a few things—I don't waste food for one thing, and I hate to see other people waste it. It made a deep impression on my habits for a long time. We saved every crumb we could.

Invariably, barracks conversations always centered on food.

"We used to sit around and talk about what we were going to eat when we got out. Our commanding officer would get tired of it and tell us to change the subject. So we'd talk about cars. Then someone would say, 'Boy! I'd like to have one with mashed potatoes and gravy all over it,'" Ivy said, laughing.

From Nuremberg, he was transferred again to Moosberg, Germany, near Munich, where he was finally liberated.

"An American tank rolled over the fence, and that was it," he said. "The last few nights the artillery was going right over our heads."

That was followed by a flight to Rheims, France, where General Alfred Jodl, chief of staff of the German High Command, signed unconditional surrender documents for all German forces to the Allies on the morning of May 7, 1945. From there, Ivy was sent to Le Havre, France, where he was evaluated medically and given all the food he could eat before sailing back home aboard a U.S. troop ship.

"I'd eat a half-chicken for lunch with malted milk and ice cream," he said. "When we waddled back into the registration center in New Jersey everybody looked at us and thought, 'Well heck, you couldn't have had it too bad.' It was more than I'd ever weighed in my life, about 165."

Ivy credits German Luftwaffe officers with making sure that American aviators were treated with at least some degree of human decency.

"They went out of their way to take good care of us," he said. "They were very protective of us. The Wehrmacht—foot soldiers—would have hammered us good if they could get their hands on us. We made out as well as could be expected."

Following his discharge, Ivy went home to Waco, Texas.

"I sat on my ass for about three weeks," he said, smiling. "Then my mother started saying, 'What are you going to do?'"

During his imprisonment, Ivy had passed the time reading Red Cross–supplied books. One of them was about how to pursue a career in advertising.

So he contacted its author, Mark O'Day, who invited him to New York and offered him a job on Madison Avenue.

Later, he became assistant director of advertising and public relations for Universal Atlas Cement Co., a subsidiary of U.S. Steel.

Through the years, he became acquainted with upstate New York, and now he and his wife, Terry, live in Schuylerville, where she runs Ivy Associates, an art gallery, at 140 Broad Street. The couple, with five grown children and four grandchildren, just marked their sixty-second anniversary on December 18.

They were married in 1946 at the famous "Little Church Around the Corner" in New York, after meeting somewhat by accident at a Greenwich Village party. "I had a date who I thought had stood me up, so I called a friend who was having a party in the village, and she said, 'Come on down! Everyone here is from Texas,'" Terry recalled. "Edwin had a date, but she was quite the buzz, surrounded by all the men, so he and I ended up talking in a corner, and he asked me to dinner the next night at the Biltmore Hotel. I was from Florida, and he was from Texas. It just seemed like a natural [fit]."

Her support and understanding proved invaluable to his successful adjustment to postwar America, worlds apart from his German captivity.

"Everywhere we went was being bombed, and the roads were being strafed," Ivy said. "Our lives were in danger all the time. It took years of reconditioning to get back to what I'd say is normal."

SONNY SEGAN: SHOT DOWN OVER EUROPE

Published November 11, 2009

Seymour "Sonny" Segan came out of Brownsville—the toughest, poorest section of Brooklyn that produced some of organized crime's most notorious figures.

Growing up in the 1920s and '30s, he heard all about the likes of Abe "Kid Twist" Reles and Jacob "Gurrah" Shapiro, members of the infamous Murder, Inc., which carried out hundreds of contract killings.

Somehow, he never fell into their world but went on to become one of America's leading businessmen, with a chain of men's clothing stores—Jonathan Reid—that made him millions. He is also a decorated American hero who flew twenty-six bombing missions over Nazi-occupied Europe and was shot down, captured and held a prisoner of war.

World War II Army Air Corps bombardier Seymour "Sonny" Segan was decorated with more than a dozen awards, including the Purple Heart, two Air Medals with an oak leaf cluster and a POW medal.

"By the way, I'm dead," Segan said, recalling the most tragic incident of his long, remarkable life. He turns eighty-seven on December 5.

On July 5, 1944, the military mistakenly informed his mother that he was missing in action. Segan had made arrangements for a telegram to only go to his father's place of business in the event that he was killed or taken prisoner. Because of the holiday weekend, however, the notice went to his house, where his mother saw it first.

"She had a cerebral hemorrhage, and she died. How do you think you feel when you find out you killed your mother?" Segan said, still fighting back tears, sixty-five years later.

His plane, a B-24 Liberator bombardier, was knocked out of the sky by an enemy fighter during a bombing run over Ploesti, Romania, whose huge oil refineries supplied the German war machine. "The plane went into a dive from thirteen thousand feet to the ground," Segan said. "I got out seconds before it hit the ground."

Suffering a shattered leg, his Romanian captors at first took him to a small civilian hospital. He was then transferred to a POW camp near Bucharest.

"At least I was with Americans, fellows I knew," he said. "We were all together."

After being held captive for more than two months, he was set free as the Russians closed in from the east and returned to Italy, where his bomber group was based. "We were the first POWs to come back to the U.S.," Segan said. "I came back to the States on a hospital ship, the USS *Refuge*. The guy on the bunk over me was Beryl 'Papa' Newman, a Medal of Honor winner."

Newman had been cited for going above and beyond the call of duty by attacking the strongly held German Anzio-Nettuno defense line near Cisterna, Italy, on May 26, 1944, in the lead of his platoon.

Segan has more than a dozen awards, too, including the Purple Heart, two Air Medals with an oak leaf cluster, a POW medal and a medal for the European, African and Middle Eastern Campaign.

A personal letter to him, dated September 4, 1944, from the Fifteenth Air Force Office of the Commanding General, says it all.

"You are going home," Major General N.F. Twining wrote.

You are the returning heroes of the Battle of Ploesti. Your safe return to my command marked the culmination of an outstanding campaign in the annals of American military history. The German war machine's disintegration on all fronts is being caused, to a large extent, by their lack of oil—oil that you took from them. I only have one regret on this jubilant occasion. I wish it had been possible to bring out of Romania every officer and man who went down in that battle.

Of the 3,781 men shot down trying to destroy Ploesti, only 1,185 came home, Segan said. Slightly built to begin with, he weighed only ninety-nine pounds at the time of his release.

"The Russians were taking over Romania, and the Germans bombed for three days and three nights," he said. "They killed more people than we did on all our missions."

Recuperating at home, recovery was slow. At one point, he was sent to the former veterans hospital atop Mount McGregor in Wilton, which introduced him to the local area. "The first pass I got, I went to Saratoga because everyone knows Saratoga," he said.

Later, he went to Glens Falls and found a supportive Jewish community, which made him feel at home.

Meanwhile, however, Segan was fighting a battle against something tougher than anything he encountered during the war—alcoholism. Returning to New York, he'd sometimes wake up in a hotel room and have to read the stationery to find out where he was, having no recollection of how he got there. An auto accident almost claimed his life.

Finally, he realized that he needed help and got it from a resource he credits with saving his life and countless others—Alcoholics Anonymous. Next March 3, he plans on celebrating fifty years of sobriety.

He and his late wife, Shirley, were married fifty-nine years and a day until her passing on November 23, 2007. Two of their three children—Scott, a doctor, and Risa, also in healthcare—went to Skidmore College, and John, whom the Jonathan Reid stores were named after, is an artist and runs the last remaining store at Aviation Mall in Queensbury.

Segan founded the men's clothing business in 1965. At its peak, the chain had seventeen stores, including one in Wilton and others from Ithaca to Massachusetts. In 1977, he was named New York State Retailer of the Year and was elected president of Menswear Retailers of America in 1990.

Wichita State University invited him to develop a business course.

"The guys who put me in charge all had MBAs," he said. "Here, I'd only taken night courses at NYU."

Among his many achievements, he is a member of the philanthropic Honorable Order of Kentucky Colonels.

"Once I sobered up, my life was great," Segan said. "I got my wife back. My wife and I worked together. We traveled to places most people don't even go. We went to China three times."

He raised his family at 552 Glen Street, Glens Falls, in a 101-year-old, eighteen-room brick mansion that includes a two-story indoor garden with a fountain and trees, a beautiful library, four fireplaces and seven bathrooms—"one for every day of the week," Segan said, laughing.

Since his boyhood at 2045 Strauss Street, where he could watch Brooklyn Dodger games from the rooftops of nearby apartment buildings, Segan has endured much and accomplished even more. "I fell in love with this area," he said. "There's something about it, coming from where I was, it was just great."

Pointing to a bedroom dresser, he read a well-known prayer: "God grant me the serenity to accept the things I cannot change, the courage to change the things I can and the wisdom to know the difference."

"I live by that," he said.

MICHAEL J. BISS: D-DAY, THE NORMANDY INVASION

Published May 28, 2001

Michael J. Biss doesn't have to see movies such as *The Longest Day* or *Saving Private Ryan* to learn about D-Day. He was there as a seaman aboard a landing ship tank, transporting a British armored division to Gold Beach as part of the Normandy Invasion.

From June 6, 1944, through November of that year, his ship made numerous shuttles between England and France carrying troops, equipment and supplies that helped turn the tide of World War II.

"I'm no hero or anything like that," the Wilton resident said. "The guys we left behind are the ones."

Biss, his brothers, John and Stephen, and their sister, Julia, each answered the call of duty during World War II, all in different branches of the service. John enlisted in the army in 1937, was reported missing on Corregidor in May 1942 and was held prisoner by the Japanese until the war's conclusion.

Julia joined the Women's Army Corps in February 1943, while Stephen signed up with the Marine Corps two months later. Michael, at age seventeen, left Saratoga Springs High School during his junior year to join the navy on Valentine's Day 1944.

A *Saratogian* article from that year featured the headline, "Biss Family Out to Avenge Brother Lost at Corregidor," with pictures of all three brothers and their sister.

Michael Biss said that his vessel was part of the third or fourth wave at Normandy, delivering its cargo several hundred yards offshore at about 10:30 a.m.

"It was just before the tide started going out," he said. "We dropped the bow as soon as the water got down to two or three feet. Tanks could drive through that."

Although by no means easy, Biss said that the British forces that went ashore at Gold Beach found much less resistance than the Americans, who assaulted Omaha and Utah Beaches.

"We traveled all night to get there," he recalled. "We weren't told anything, but we figured it out. The planes were going like mad."

Biss's landing ship tank no. 2, nicknamed *Duce*, returned to England after delivering its payload and came back to Normandy at Sword Beach on June 8. This time, it took four direct hits from heavy German guns, and the entire crew of 120 seamen had to abandon ship. *Duce* was later recovered and put back into action after the fighting quieted down.

"I had shrapnel go all around me and didn't get hit. Without thinking, I took cover under an ammo supply," he said with a laugh. "If it had gotten hit, I would have been a goner. But we lost no crew members."

Biss joined his ship in May 1944, fresh out of boot camp, after traveling across the Atlantic on the *Queen Mary* with five hundred other sailors, bound for Scotland and then Southampton, England.

"When I went aboard, I was nothing but a raw recruit," he said.

Ironically, after surviving D-Day, he didn't go through amphibious training until returning stateside in December and reporting to Fort Pierce, Florida, on the USS *Kenosha*. Biss hoped for a Pacific tour, but it never came through.

"Hey, you're young," he said. "I grew up fast, though. If I had to do it over again, I'd do it again. You met a lot of nice guys."

Since 1989, members of the landing ship tank no. 2 have been holding annual reunions, most of which Biss has attended. His car even bears a special license plate that reads "Duce, USLST2, June 6, 1944."

He was discharged on March 7, 1946, came home and went to work at American Locomotive Co. in Schenectady before taking over his parents' Route 50 farm. Biss has always thought about returning to Normandy but just hasn't taken the time to do it.

Perhaps he simply thinks that once was enough.

"I'll never forget it," he said.

CLARENCE DART: TUSKEGEE AIRMAN

Published April 19, 1996

Clarence Dart of Saratoga Springs might never have made ninety-five fighter pilot missions during World War II if it weren't for Charles A. "Chief" Anderson. None of the 450 black pilots in the U.S. Army Air Corps would have gotten their wings if Anderson hadn't paved the way for them.

Anderson, eighty-nine, who died recently, was considered the father of black aviation. He learned to fly by reading books and getting tips from young white pilots, obtaining his license in 1929. Later, he trained the Tuskegee Airmen, America's first black military pilots, including Dart.

"He was just an ordinary person but very competent because he taught himself to fly," said Dart, seventy-five. "He was instrumental in getting black people admitted to training in the air corps."

Anderson was assisted in his efforts by Eleanor Roosevelt, who visited Tuskegee University in Alabama in 1940. He took her on a flight to disprove a mistaken notion that blacks did not make good aviators.

Dart was drafted in 1942 and started out in a field artillery unit at Fort Sill, Oklahoma, until he was able to join pilots school. He trained at Tuskegee from February to November 1943, when he was commissioned as a second lieutenant.

He said that Anderson was the school's chief administrator and that much of the actual training was done by white instructors.

Clarence Dart of Saratoga Springs was a pioneering aviator with the Tuskegee Airmen, an African American U.S. Army Air Corps unit during World War II.

"They were great," he said. "They gave us the best training possible. But early on, some of the higher-ups, they were the problem. They never could come to grips with the situation. There was still resistance to black people being trained as pilots in the military. There was quite a bit of opposition."

Dart, who grew up in Elmira, was surprised by his first taste of the Deep South.

"I grew up in an integrated neighborhood," he said. "The kids played ball together. All black kids had heard about Jim Crow laws in the South. To encounter it personally was kind of a shock."

But he made it through the school and was assigned to the Ninety-ninth Fighter Squadron in the Twelfth Air Force, starting out in North Africa in January 1944. Flying a P-40, he made forty-five successful missions, dive-bombing and strafing enemy soldiers in close support of Allied troops.

Later, his squadron moved into Italy, where it took on new responsibilities. Manning a P-51, Dart began escorting Fifteenth Air Force bombers as they made round trips, up to seven hours long, hitting targets from Germany to Greece.

"We took them all the way from the target back to the base," he said. "The Germans were sending fighters up in their own flak to shoot down our bombers, so we'd be right in the flak with them."

Most of his flights started on Italy's Adriatic coast, due east of Naples. "The engineers would go in and scrape out a runway," he said.

He recalled encountering German ME-262 jets for the first time when he was over Berlin in one of his last missions in April 1945. "You couldn't touch them because they were so fast," he said.

Despite his heroics, Dart said that press reports at the time criticized black pilots as being afraid to fly or guilty of hitting wrong targets.

"Which wasn't true," he said.

The role of African Americans in U.S. military history has often gone overlooked, Dart said. "In every war the U.S. has fought, blacks have been involved," he said.

Crispus Attucks was the first Patriot to die in the American Revolution, and more than 180,000 blacks—many of them former slaves—fought for the Union during the Civil War.

Dart took a job with General Electric Co. in Schenectady after World War II and made Saratoga Springs his permanent home. From GE, he went to Knolls Atomic Power Lab in Niskayuna, where he rose to senior engineer before retiring in 1987. However, he continued his military career in the reserves, attaining the rank of lieutenant colonel before retiring in 1985.

He said that Anderson remained active as a pilot well into his eighties and lost his license because of medical reasons only a few years ago—and Dart is one of many men who remember him fondly.

Congressional Gold Medal

In March 2007, Dart was among the Tuskegee Airmen honored in Washington, D.C., with a Congressional Gold Medal—the highest civilian award Congress can bestow.

Along with the award, Dart received an American flag that flew over the Capitol Building from U.S. representative Kirsten Gillibrand.

"Clarence is an American hero, and I'm thrilled he's been awarded the Congressional Gold Medal," Gillibrand said. "Clarence's story is an inspiration. We can learn from his patriotism, perseverance and strength of character."

Joined by his wife, Millie, three of his eight children—Denise, Dawn and Rose Anne—and one of his grandsons, Keith, Dart traveled to Washington, D.C., to receive his honor. "I'm so proud of my father," said daughter Joyce Dart from their home in Saratoga Springs. "I can't wait until he gets home so I can see the medal and congratulate him. This is long overdue."

President George W. Bush, members of Congress and other dignitaries joined the airmen, widows and other relatives in the Capitol Rotunda for the ceremony recognizing the Tuskegee Airmen—some of them walking with the aid of canes, others being pushed in wheelchairs—for their long-ago heroism.

"I thought it was great that the president saluted them," said Denise, who watched the ceremony with others on closed-circuit TV because the rotunda was packed with honorees.

The Tuskegee Airmen were recruited into an Army Air Corps program that trained blacks to fly and maintain combat aircraft. Most military leaders at the time were against the squadron's formation. "They considered Tuskegee an experiment at best and an unwarranted political intrusion at worst," said Colonel John D. Silvera, the airmen's national public relations officer.

However, President Franklin D. Roosevelt overruled his top generals and ordered the program's creation. Nearly one thousand fighter pilots trained as a segregated unit at an air base in Tuskegee, Alabama. Not allowed to practice or fight alongside their white counterparts, the Tuskegee Airmen distinguished themselves by painting the tails of their airplanes red, which resulted in their being known as the "Red Tails."

Hundreds saw combat throughout Europe, the Mediterranean and North Africa, escorting bomber aircraft on missions and protecting them from the enemy. Dozens died in the fighting; others were held as prisoners of war. "When they didn't fail, they found that they had earned the respect of their white comrades," Silvera said.

Dart was shot down twice, once in April 1944 just north of Rome and again two months later over Anzio. After serving overseas, he returned to Tuskegee as an instructor and spent the remainder of his service as a squadron commander.

"We thought because we'd demonstrated we could do anything anyone else could do, there would be big changes," he said. "But as soon as peace came, we saw there had not been."

However, the armed services was finally integrated in 1948.

"The fact that we did succeed opened the door for a lot of people in the air force," Dart said. "The chance to fly was the dream of anyone who became a Tuskegee Airman."

BILL BOYLE: WEST POINT GRADUATE, AIRBORNE

Published June 25, 2007

Bill Boyle earned a Distinguished Service Cross and two Purple Hearts in World War II, followed by combat action in Korea. A 1939 West Point graduate, he served under some of the most famous leaders in U.S. military history before retiring in 1967 during the early stages of the Vietnam War.

This week, he'll be traveling to Washington, D.C., for a reunion of the 517th Parachute Regimental Combat Team, which fought throughout Europe from Rome to the Rhineland during the Second World War. A lieutenant colonel, Boyle was the group's commanding officer.

"It affects different people differently," said Boyle of Saratoga Springs, reflecting on his military training. "In my case, it made me consider the people under me as well as the people over me. Probably I'm alive because of it."

In January 1945, after jumping into the Battle of the Bulge, he took a burst of machine-gun fire while out on night patrol. Nerves in both arms were damaged, and a major artery was severed. Three other soldiers were with Boyle, and he told them to leave him and rejoin the fight, expecting to die shortly anyway.

"The problem with you, colonel," one of the men barked, "is that you haven't got the guts to help yourself."

Both taken aback and challenged by the rebuke, Boyle got up and got going with the soldier's help, which he credits for saving his life.

"He got me to my feet and half carried me back to the command post," Boyle said. "I've never seen that man since."

But he hasn't forgotten and never will.

Only days beforehand, on Christmas Day 1944, Boyle risked his life by walking directly into intense fire from a friendly battalion that was mistakenly shooting at men under his command.

He kept advancing, without protection, until his group's safety was ensured. His extraordinary courage saved numerous American lives and earned Boyle the Distinguished Service Cross, one of the military's highest honors.

A Brooklyn native, Boyle got into West Point somewhat by accident. He was told in March of his senior year in high school that appointments had already been filled, but following Mass each Sunday morning, he went to visit his congressman with hopes of gaining entry.

"Two days before the entrance exam I got a message to report to 24 Whitehall Street in Manhattan, where the army had an installation," he said. "To my surprise, I passed."

In early 1937, while still a cadet, he marched down Pennsylvania Avenue in President Franklin D. Roosevelt's second inaugural parade.

"It was a cold, rainy day," he said, exhibiting an extremely sharp mind that betrays his years.

Boyle's age? "High eighty-nine," he said, laughing.

He and his wife, Babbie, had ten children and celebrated their sixtieth anniversary on June 21, proud to have twenty grandchildren and several great-grandchildren. The couple met after the war at Fort Sheridan, Illinois, where Babbie's father, Major General Lewis Craig, was the Fifth Army's deputy commanding general. Her grandfather, General Malin Craig, was army chief of staff from 1935 to 1939 and chaired the War Department's personnel board throughout World War II.

Five straight generations on her side of the family have graduated from West Point.

She was a self-described "army brat" who moved wherever her father went, while Boyle's boyhood roots were firmly established in Brooklyn, where he was a Dodgers fan who saved the fifty-five cents for an Ebbets Field bleacher seat by watching games through the outfield fence. An accomplished athlete, he won medals at the famous Millrose Games, America's oldest track-and-field event.

He described his first day at West Point as a "shock to the system."

"It was always tougher when I was there," he said, chuckling. "They always think that way."

After graduation, he was sent to the Panama Canal Zone, making twice-weekly trips through the canal. On December 7, 1941, he was stationed at Fort Benning, Georgia, when he learned about the Japanese attack on Pearl Harbor.

"The professor of economics when I was a cadet predicted that we would be fighting Japan some day," Boyle said. "It was a case of the 'haves' and 'have-nots.' Japan was a 'have-not.'"

The 517th parachute team saw its first action in Italy, and Boyle was wounded for the first time on Monte Peloso, where mortar fragments hit him in the leg. Later, the outfit moved up through southern France.

After being severely wounded, he was sent back to the United States in March 1945 and spent twenty-one months in a Staten Island hospital.

Following his military retirement, Boyle ran a tax and accounting service and moved to Saratoga Springs in 1972; he and his wife are surrounded by many of their children and grandchildren.

A decorated veteran who served his country with distinction, he can't wait to meet with old friends and war buddies this week in the nation's capital.

When asked what he's most proud of, however, Boyle responded without hesitation.

"My family," he said.

MORRIS KATZ: EYES IN THE SKY

Published November 9, 2008

Morris Katz had a bird's-eye view of World War II and saved countless American lives with cutting-edge technology that helped shape the war's outcome.

The eighty-seven-year-old Wilton resident flew more than one hundred missions as a B-24 bomber radar operator, hunting for German submarines

Morris Katz flew more than one hundred missions as a B-24 bomber radar operator, hunting for German submarines during World War II.

that threatened to blow up troop ships crossing the Atlantic with upwards of five thousand soldiers on board.

Katz was part of the first class of U.S. airmen to learn about airborne radar—a highly classified development—prior to America's entry into the war.

"I mean secret," he said. "The Germans didn't know it. No one knew it."

The technology was invented by the British, who shared it in exchange for America's role in the Lend Lease Program, in which the United States supplied destroyers for Britain's war effort. Seeing conflict on the horizon, Katz enlisted in the Army Air Corps in August 1940—earning twenty-one-dollars per month—and later went to Canada to train with RAF flyers.

From there, his group headed to MIT in Boston for additional instruction. The first American airborne radar was made by Raytheon Corporation and fit onto the aircraft's nose, providing a 360-degree view of objects in the water below.

The principle was simple: search and destroy, or at least keep German subs below the surface where they couldn't inflict any damage.

Beneath the waves, subs could only travel ten to twelve knots, versus twenty or more on top. Those that came up risked the possibility of an aerial attack and certain destruction.

The nose of Katz's bomber was marked with a swastika for each kill or hit. Normally flying at up to three thousand feet, during attacks the plane would drop to just above the surface to deliver depth charges with maximum firepower.

Katz's job, when engaging the enemy, was to make sure that depth charges cleared the plane and didn't get hung up in the bomb bay. That vantage point gave him a bird's-eye view, and the visual imprint of one direct hit is still with him to this day.

"The whole tail end of the sub was sticking out of the water," he said.

To start with, Katz's crew spent five months flying off the U.S. coast, from New York to Key West, responding to scares about German submarine sightings. He remembers one incident off Jacksonville, Florida, in which a tanker was sunk in broad daylight.

Eventually, he was sent overseas, taking a southern route across the Atlantic by way of Central and South America before heading to West Africa and up the coast to England. The journey included a mid-Atlantic stop at Ascension Island, a brutally remote outpost whose confining conditions, cut off from the outside world, tested the limits of servicemen stationed there.

It's just one example of the little-known suffering that young Americans endured during the war without much fanfare or glory.

"The troops are the people I feel so much compassion for, the GIs who really had to go through blood and guts," Katz said. "They really slugged it out. I feel guilty myself sometimes because I had a great job. I love adventure. That's how I survived, I guess, because I loved what I was doing."

Katz spent most of the war stationed in former French West Africa, where he flew patrols from five hundred to one thousand miles out over the ocean. "Twenty-four hours a day, day and night, we were out there to keep those subs down so they wouldn't get our troop ships," he said. "Not one of those big ships like the *Queen Mary* was ever sunk."

The crew consisted of a pilot, copilot, engineer and assistant, radio operator and assistant, navigator, bombardier, gunnery man and Katz—the radar operator. One time, Katz said, the pilot and copilot flipped a coin to see who would fly the plane

"They were all fresh, right out of training," he said. "I had more hours than all of them combined. I was the leader of the crew that I was on."

Race or religion didn't matter—Arab, Jew, Catholic or Protestant.

"We had everything you could think of," Katz said. "Air crews are very close-knit. You're like a family."

One of his guiding life principles is that a man's love is only as deep as his willingness to suffer on someone else's behalf. German bombers were also on the hunt for U.S. ships, and Katz's crew, putting their own lives at risk, would sometimes engage them in midair combat.

"We would get into dogfights out there," he said. "We didn't have to do that, because we were supposed to be looking for submarines. I guess that was part of our esprit de corps."

Or selflessness and sacrifice—traits that have characterized his family and his wife Natalie's for generations. Her father, Stanley Garner, won a Purple Heart in World War I and was elected to Virginia's House of Delegates.

She lost two brothers to military service. Selwyn Garner, a navy gunner, suffered a fatal aviation accident during World War II, and another brother, Gordon, was killed in the Korean War after thirteen years in the marines.

"We're a highly military-oriented type of family," Katz said. "Very patriotic."

Whether from accidents or enemy fire, the United States lost half of all its airborne antisubmarine crews, Katz said. One time, with his plane heavily laden down with ammunition, he miraculously survived a crash during a failed takeoff.

Having logged nearly seven hundred hours of flight time, he is quietly proud of his military honors, which include an Air Medal with three oak leaf clusters—the equivalent of four Air Medals.

Katz returned home to the United States in November 1944 and finished out the war instructing new crews at Langley Field in Virginia. Natalie, whom he hadn't met yet, was still going to school at James Madison University in Harrisonburg, Virginia. One weekend, Katz was supposed to meet her on a blind date but couldn't keep it because of another German submarine scare.

About a year later, she went to a USO dance with a friend, but upon arriving, they discovered that it had been canceled. By total coincidence, the girls bumped into a pair of young servicemen, and one of them was Katz. Fate, evidently, was determined to bring them together. After they were married, Morris and Natalie learned through a mutual friend that they had been each other's intended date on the blind date that couldn't be kept.

Settling in Briarcliff Manor, near Katz's native Ossining, they began raising a family before finding a dream home on Saratoga Lake, which had been built by former Saratoga Race Course starter Mars Cassidy. In years past, Cassidy had entertained the likes of Bing Crosby there, one of many famous celebrities who visited the Spa City during the mid-twentieth century.

The couple, married sixty-two years now, has since moved to Wilton and has three grown sons, six grandchildren and five great-grandchildren. Once a year, the Katzes hold a reunion that's humorously referred to as a gathering of the "Empire."

One time, someone mistakenly phoned Katz, trying to find an army officer with the exact same first and last names.

"Is this General Morris Katz?" the caller asked.

"No, but I'm the emperor of the Empire," Katz said, laughing.

IWO JIMA: MARINE CORPS MEMORIES

Published November 10, 2007

The image of U.S. Marines raising the American flag at Iwo Jima's Mount Suribachi inspired a war-weary nation to victory over Japan. To Ballston Spa's Al Harris, it meant nothing; at least, not at the time.

He had already stormed the blood-soaked beaches of Saipan and Tinian and watched thousands of fellow Fourth Division marines fall to Japanese fire. Unlike the World Series or Super Bowl, such battles weren't followed by wild celebrations or downtown parades.

"I never knew the famous picture had been taken," Harris said. "I don't remember any happy events. We went in, you're there, you're gone. It wasn't

U.S. Marines (left to right) Fred Bessette and Tom Morrissey of Clifton Park, Sal Fanularo of Glenville and Al Harris of Ballston Spa were part of the battle for Iwo Jima in World War II.

until after the war and I started reading that I realized what an impact the flag raising had."

He and three other Iwo Jima veterans were among those gathered at American Legion Post 1450 on Saturday to celebrate the Marine Corps' 232nd birthday. It wasn't a large group, about fifteen or so, but the stories, laughter and camaraderie were worth their weight in gold.

"When they planted the second flag the guy [Associated Press photographer Joe Rosenthal] just caught a great picture," said Harris, of K Company, Third Battalion, Twenty-fourth Regiment Marines. "It's the most outstanding picture from World War II, something that will last forever. It's something that everybody of every age group can identify with. You couldn't stage anything like that. If you staged something like that it wouldn't come out good."

Harris had already advanced about a mile forward of Mount Suribachi and was on the front lines when the U.S. flag went up. Just raising his head to look back meant risking his life, because twenty-three thousand Japanese were dug in all over the three- by five-mile volcanic island.

"By the time we landed, none of them were above ground," he said. "I never saw a live Japanese. They fought from cave mouths, and there were caves connected throughout the island."

Clifton Park's Tom Morrissey and Fred Bessette and Glenville's Sal Fanularo were there, too.

"We served with the finest group of men you'd ever want to meet in your life," Morrissey said. "We all watched out for each other, we all protected each other. We wouldn't leave a marine behind. If we could walk or crawl, we'd take him with us. That was the most important thing, to save each other. I'm proud to be in the United States Marines."

"I lasted eleven days," Bessette said. "That was pretty good longevity. I'm just glad to have gotten off the thing."

Seven thousand Americans didn't.

"I think back every once in a while, and I don't know how I ever got through it," Fanularo said.

The Iwo Jima flag raising has generated considerable debate in recent years, because those pictured gained worldwide fame and adoration. The flag Rosenthal photographed was the second one marines raised, however. A previous one was put up less dramatically, and those who took part have never been recognized. In fact, some weren't even invited to the Marine Corps monument's dedication in Washington, D.C.

"That's the way of the world," Harris said.

Sixty-two years after the horrific battle, he is unconvinced that Iwo Jima was even necessary. Strategically, the island had airfields from which American bombers could take off to make raids over Japan.

"The planes couldn't make it back to Saipan," Morrissey said.

"Every time the B-29s would take off from the Marianas, they would get harassed on the way going over to bomb Japan," Fanularo added. "That's fifteen hundred miles. Coming back, the ones that were crippled, they didn't make it back because the Jap fighters just knocked them out of the sky."

"Maybe it saved a few," Harris said of the victory at Iwo Jima. "But you'd have to save a helluva lot to make up for seven thousand people [Americans] killed. In retrospect, we could have stopped at Saipan, bombed the Japanese the way we did and that's all we would have had to do. We didn't have to take Okinawa or any of those. A lot of bad decisions were made."

At Normandy, U.S. soldiers came under attack the second they hit the beach. At Iwo Jima, the Japanese let marines come ashore before opening fire.

"It was like putting twenty thousand people on a nine-hole golf course," Harris said. "Any time the Japanese fired, they were going to hit or kill somebody."

Fanularo said that the Japanese were so well fortified that "not even a rat could get through."

"Allied commanders could have and should have avoided the bloodbath that unfolded," Harris said. "We had napalm and we had the bombers and we could have taken it with no losses, because the fire would have sucked all the air out of the caves. But we were still on the moral high ground, and they weren't considering that."

Six months later, the United States dropped atomic bombs on Hiroshima and Nagasaki, bringing the war to an almost immediate conclusion.

Two years ago, Harris went back to Saipan to show his son, Dan, where he'd fought and witnessed indescribable hardships. The beaches were barely recognizable, looking more like a South Pacific paradise than a tangle of dead and dying American heroes.

The first time he was there, hundreds of islanders had jumped off steep cliffs to their deaths, fearful of Americans because of what the Japanese had told them. This time, Harris was greeted warmly, making his trip back through time worth every mile.

The experience brought everything about being a marine into perspective.

"Thank you for freeing us," they told him.

"I never had such a day in my life," he said.

KOREAN WAR

REMEMBERING THE FORGOTTEN WAR

Published May 15, 2009

The Korean War was the first clash between superpowers during a Cold War that lasted more than forty years. The Berlin Wall, the Cuban Missile Crisis, the Space Race, Vietnam and the nuclear arms buildup were all part of the ongoing struggle.

If the United States hadn't intervened in Korea, communism would have gone unchecked throughout Asia, and Soviet dominance, rather than democracy, would have prevailed in Europe, veterans say.

"Communism was meant to spread throughout the Far East, and we stopped them in Korea," said Jim Ferris, national first vice-president of Korean War Veterans of America. "Otherwise, the people of South Korea, Japan and the rest of the Far East would be under communist control."

"That's why Korean people today are so appreciative of what we did," said Irv Breitbart, state commander, Korean War Veterans of New York. The group held its (2009) spring conference at Longfellow's Hotel & Conference Center with more than one hundred members on hand. The event was organized by local veterans Gene Corsale, Ray Waldron and Lincoln Orologio.

"I'm together with people who walked the walk and understand," said Ernest Benson of Greenport, Long Island.

He was a spotter, a radio sergeant forward observer with the Seventh Infantry Division's Thirty-first Field Artillery, which manned 155-caliber

Howitzers. "I was over there fourteen months from 1952 to early 1953," he said. "The worst engagement was Jane Russell Hill. That was the official name. It was two knobs."

Today, he can smile at the name. Back then, it was pure hell.

"The battle lines kept changing," he said. "We were in North Korea about fifty miles north of the thirty-eighth parallel. It was a very significant battle known as the 'Hill Fights,' along with Sniper's Ridge and Triangle Hill, an area called the Iron Triangle."

During one exchange, an enemy mortar hit the trench he was in.

"Most of the injured landed on top of me," he said. "I was unconscious. They thought I was dead."

Benson's left hand took a piece of mortar shrapnel, and his lieutenant promised to put him in for a Purple Heart when they returned home. "He never got back," he said. "That was the end of that."

Benson has suffered from post-traumatic stress syndrome ever since Korea, one of the unseen injuries that plague countless veterans. Like other soldiers from the "Forgotten War," his battle isn't done.

"I'm also active in The American Legion," he said. "I help other veterans negotiate through benefits they might not know about otherwise. I steer them and put them on the right path."

To Ferris, who's in line to become Korean War Veterans' national commander, the fight is altogether different.

"They can forget the war if they want to," he said. "But don't forget the 54,000 who died there and the 108,000 wounded in action."

The former marine was in Korea from 1952 to '53, assigned to coordinate operations between the First and Third Divisions.

Breitbart, an army veteran, visits schools whenever possible to teach young people what the war was all about. "If it wasn't for us at that time, it would have changed all history," he said.

He added, however, that the United States was ill prepared and ill equipped to fight when hostilities broke out on June 25, 1950. The first U.S. troops to respond were part of a peacekeeping occupation force in Japan, stationed in the island nation following the end of World War II five years earlier.

Most weren't combat ready and didn't have sufficient rations or proper clothing to deal with the frigid Korean winter.

"The first year of the war we lost a tremendous amount of people," Ferris said.

"But the guys were proud to serve," Breitbart said.

Three years later, a truce was declared, "ending a war that technically isn't over," Benson said.

Unlike their older friends and brothers, who were greeted as heroes after World War II, a silent reception greeted Korean War veterans. "We came home very quietly," Ferris said. "We went back to work, we went back to school."

"There was no one at the docks waiting for us," Breitbart said. "We didn't get the greeting the people coming back from Iraq and Afghanistan are getting."

Today, more than fifty years later, North Korea is still a source of tension on the world stage with the government's ongoing threat to develop missiles with nuclear capability. In the eyes of Americans who fought there, the United States needs to remain vigilant to keep history from repeating itself.

"They don't know anything but firmness," Ferris said. "You can't play games with them."

GENE CORSALE: VETERAN OF THE YEAR

Published November 11, 2008

Korean War veteran Gene Corsale has been named the New York Military Heritage Institute's Veteran of the Year. Corsale, eighty, was a petty officer, second class, in the U.S. Navy from 1950 to 1954, with forty-five months of sea duty on the battleship USS *Wisconsin* and the aircraft carrier USS *Midway*.

The Spa City resident has been a strong promoter of veterans programs and activities throughout his adult life. He was honored Saturday during ceremonies at the New York State Military Museum with Major General Joseph Taluto, adjutant general of New York, and institute president Fred Altman in attendance.

"It makes you very humble," Corsale said. "I think about all the guys that didn't come back. What we try to do is honor their memory. I'm very happy that a Korean War veteran was chosen for this honor. We were the forgotten veterans from the 'Forgotten War.'"

He and his wife, Barbara, have two daughters and four grandchildren.

Among his accomplishments, Corsale has co-chaired Saratoga County's Deceased Veteran of the Month program for the past nine years, was instrumental in the restoration of St. Peter's World War II memorial, has

Gene Corsale of Saratoga Springs has been an active advocate for veterans for many years. He was in the navy during the Korean War.

worked with the Albany-Saratoga submarine group on annual programs, was past vice commander of Adirondack Post 60 Korean War Veterans of America, was a trustee member of the Military Heritage Institute and was a member of the Italian-American War Veterans.

He has also worked with the institute's oral history unit by building a videotape file of the county's deceased veteran program. Earlier this year, he helped place one of the nation's first plaques—located at Railroad Place and Division Street—honoring those who have served in Iraq, Afghanistan and the War on Terror.

Corsale was Saratoga County's real property tax director for twenty years. In that position, he lobbied for state legislation for preservation and enhancement of veterans real property tax exemptions. He also assisted veterans and their widows in applying for and preparing veterans real property tax exemptions.

"The veteran's motto is, 'First military service, then service to country,'" he said.

Corsale managed a project at the 196-year-old Gideon Putnam Cemetery in Saratoga Springs that involved restoration of Civil War and Revolutionary War veterans' plots. In one special instance, he helped family and relatives

Korean War veteran Gene Corsale of Saratoga Springs was named 2008 New York Military Heritage Institute's Veteran of the Year.

have their loved one—a deceased World War II veteran—moved from a national cemetery on Long Island to Saratoga National Cemetery so that his final resting place could be a local one.

Previous recipients of the institute's Veteran of the Year award are Major Paul Hillman and Colonel John Edwards, part of America's greatest generation.

"It's an honor to be mentioned in the same breath with them," Corsale said.

The USS *Wisconsin* was part of the navy's Seventh Fleet during the Korean War.

"We shelled the coastline of Korea," he said. "We got hit, too, by shore batteries."

He also served in the Mediterranean aboard the *Midway* in the Sixth Fleet.

Corsale's late brothers, Francis "Lefty" and Dennis, served in the army and U.S. Coast Guard, respectively. Francis flew in Piper Cubs as an artillery observer during World War II. Dennis was a first-class signalman on a patrol frigate.

"A person can make no greater statement than that of, 'I am a veteran, I have served my country, I have met my commitment to country,'" Corsale said. "A veteran is someone who at one point in his or her life wrote a blank check, payable to the United States of America, for an amount up to and including my life. That is honor, that is a patriot, that is a veteran."

DONALD C. PORTER: WOUNDED THREE TIMES

Published November 11, 2005

On Veterans Day, Don Porter's thoughts always go back to Korea, where he earned three Purple Hearts and escaped capture twice as a U.S. Marine. This year, the welfare of his grandson, Chris Rathbun, also weighs heavily on his mind, because the young Fort Ann resident is awaiting deployment to Iraq.

Porter, seventy-one, was fifteen when he stole his older brother's birth certificate and joined the army in 1949. Two years later, he entered the marines and was sent overseas—fifty-two years ago this month.

"He loves his country," said his wife, Carol. "I'm proud of him, and I'm glad what they did for our country. If it wasn't for them, the country wouldn't be what it is."

Porter has a vast wealth of stories about his military life. Unfortunately, he can't share them, the result of a stroke he suffered two days after returning from a 1996 trip to see the Korean War Veterans Memorial in Washington, D.C.

The memorial features life-sized sculptures of soldiers in a combat scene, which Carol Porter believes triggered her husband's ailment.

"That was very emotional," she said.

Their grandson is in the army, previously served in Kosovo and was recently called back to active duty. At the last report, he would be going to Al Basrah, a city just north of Kuwait in southeast Iraq.

"It's scary, very scary," Carol Porter said.

Her husband survived many harrowing experiences, but like many soldiers, he never talked about them. Although fully alert and active with a keen sense of humor, he's unable to communicate verbally.

A scrapbook with dozens of old photos from his service days provides some insight into what life must have been like in Korea. One picture shows

Porter standing in front of a makeshift tent, looking a bit bedraggled with his shirttails hanging out.

On the back, he wrote, "Don't laugh. We just got done marching for the second time."

His key chain includes a tiny can opener from his marine days and a jagged, one-and-a-half-inch piece of shrapnel that doctors pulled out of his midsection.

"Our oldest granddaughter used to tell him he had two belly buttons," Carol Porter said, laughing. "He was wounded three times. Once in the leg, once in the thigh and once up in the stomach."

A sergeant, he was also taken prisoner by the enemy and suffered torture before escaping to freedom. Details are sketchy, but he said in the past that he got away by floating downriver on a log.

"They don't come any tougher than this man here," said Jeff Johnson, the family's full-time caregiver.

In 1984, Carol Porter was inflicted by a rare spinal virus that left her confined to a wheelchair. For the next dozen years, Don built devices to make her home life easier. Washington County Public Health officials took notice and asked if he'd do the same for others in need.

"They'd go to pay him, and he'd say, 'Nope, you get the material and I'll do it,'" Carol said.

Then he suffered a stroke, which left both of them in need of assistance. Fortunately, they're still able to enjoy a comfortable, log-style home off Buttermilk Falls Road in rural West Fort Ann.

A colorful American flag with the Marine Corps logo greets visitors, and inside, the Porter household is a mini-museum of marine memorabilia.

"There's no military like the Marine Corps," Carol Porter said.

Don sports a bright red jacket with a large Korean War Veterans patch on the back. When he touches the bill of his cap, the Marine Corps hymn starts to play, evoking a round of happy laughter.

He plans on attending Veterans Day services in Glens Falls, and he's a regular at monthly meetings of a local Korean War Veterans chapter.

Among other things, the veterans group sends care packages to U.S. soldiers in Iraq, and Don also belongs to the Marine Corps League and Veterans of Foreign Wars.

"He does a lot," Johnson said. "He rides the stationary bike each morning and does arm exercises. He dusts, he polishes, he mows the lawn. When we go out for breakfast, he knows everybody. He could be elected mayor of West Fort Ann."

Donald C. Porter passed away on February 7, 2010. Adirondack Chapter 60 Korean War Veterans of America created the Sergeant Donald C. Porter U.S. Marine Corps Memorial, recognition that will be given to a deserving chapter member each year at the organization's annual gathering.

COLD WAR

JOHN TOTTEN: IRON CURTAIN BORDER GUARD

Previously unpublished

The Germany that John Totten found was much different from the one the Allies defeated in World War II. The Saratoga Springs resident spent about eighteen months doing border patrol duty near the town of Bindlach, close to Nurnberg, where the Iron Curtain divided the country in half between West and East Germany.

"I got my draft notice on my twentieth birthday—March 27, 1953," he said. "The Korean War was still on. I did sixteen weeks of infantry basic training at Fort Dix. I can still remember the day—we were doing .30-caliber machine-gun training—we were interrupted to announce that the Korean War had ended. The company commander said, 'I don't care what religion you are. Get down on your knees. The war is over.'"

Totten grew up in the Spa City delivering newspapers for *The Saratogian*. He later joined its production department and has been with the newspaper more than fifty years. So naturally, when he arrived in Germany in October 1953, he interviewed for an apprenticeship with *Stars & Stripes* military newspaper.

"Then I finally got my orders—AC. I thought that was the air corps. I didn't know where I was going or what I was walking into," he said, laughing.

In reality, "AC" stood for armored cavalry, and before he knew it, Totten found himself at the Seventh Army Tank Training Center in Vilseck, Germany, which graduated more than ten thousand men between 1948,

John Totten (above) came face to face with the Iron Curtain as a tank operator and border guard in West Germany during the mid-1950s.

when it opened, and 1954, when he got through there. The former German training center was the only tank school in Europe for NATO and U.S. forces.

In the turret mechanics course, students were taught turret familiarization, machine-gun assembly, bore sighting, zeroing procedure and handling of tank ammunition. Soldiers were also taught how to drive, command and fire the tank's guns.

"That's why I don't hear good today," Totten said.

He quickly picked up on tank driving, which is done with levers—no steering wheel—because he'd never driven a car before entering the service and didn't have to relearn the skill. He grew up in downtown Saratoga Springs.

"Not many people had cars," he said. "We walked everywhere."

Totten's tank was an M41, known as the "Walker Bulldog," named after General W.W. Walker, who was killed in a jeep accident in Korea. It was a light tank, with speeds up to forty-five miles per hour, equipped with a 76mm main gun, an M2 .50-caliber machine gun and a .30-caliber machine gun. Highly maneuverable, the tank had a four-man crew.

Despite such training, Totten spent a good share of time at an observation post watching border activities.

"We weren't allowed to get within fifty meters of the fence," he said.

You could see East German border guards on the other side. We'd go out on border patrol with a half-track. The tank was back at your company area in case you needed it. Most of the time you were looking through binoculars to see if anything was going on. Anything out of the ordinary, you'd call it in.

It wasn't really dangerous, but still it was something that had to be done. It was just like the border between North and South Korea. You just stood there looking.

It was a strange feeling for soldiers to stand at the edge of the Iron Curtain. Unlike any other boundary, it marked a dividing line between two utterly different ways of life. Members of the Second Cavalry took pride in knowing that they stood guard for freedom.

U.S. troops lived in old German army barracks near the border and took turns doing night or day twelve-hour rotating-guard-duty shifts.

"You're in the dark all night, and no cigarettes because they'd see where you were," Totten said. "There were some instances when roving border patrols were fired upon."

Those incidents were rare, however. For the most part, border patrol meant weariness, bad weather and long hours.

Of all his experiences, winter maneuvers were the worst.

"They'd wait for the cold weather, then they'd take you out for cold-weather indoctrination," he said.

In July 1954, he graduated from the Seventh Army's Noncommissioned Officer Academy in Munich, a five-week class dealing with everything from leadership to map reading. Of course, there was some time for fun amidst the work.

"That's where I saw my first outdoor beer garden," Totten said, smiling.

He recalls being particularly impressed by the Autobahn, the world's first superhighway that was built for military purposes. Aircraft, he said, could land and taxi off the road into secluded hiding spots under hills.

The Autobahn impressed General Dwight Eisenhower so much that he patterned America's interstate highway system after it during his time as president.

The Autobahn A9 passed through an old part of Bindlach, separating it from newer sections built during the 1950s, '60s and '70s.

For the most part, Totten found German people friendly to American troops, although many towns and villages still had vivid reminders of World War II's devastation.

"They treated you very well," Totten said.

It was extremely important for the Second Cavalry to maintain good relations with Germany's civilian population, which was important to the country's reestablishment as a sovereign power. Soldiers took part in charitable projects such as parties for underprivileged children. Likewise, German locals were invited to military parades, celebrations and similar activities. The regiment showed that it could not only defeat an enemy but also win friends.

Years later, after returning home, Totten got a Christmas card and letter from an acquaintance he'd made in Germany.

"Are you still a soldier?" the friend asked. "If you come to Germany again we would be glad to have you come and visit us. There is a lot of building going on, especially road construction toward the Iron Curtain. The tension right now all along the border is unpleasant. Don't let's get worried about this...So I will close."

Archaeological excavations indicate that the area around Bindlach was settled as early as 1300 BC, during the Bronze Age. Its first mention in modern times was in a private charter dated April 1178, and it became part of the Kingdom of Bavaria in 1810.

The large American military base where Totten lived was to the east of Bindlach on top of hills overlooking town. Officially called Christtensen Barracks, soldiers who stayed there called it the Rock.

Its main function was to secure the borders of West Germany and Czechoslovakia—about forty-three miles away. The Second Armored Cavalry made its home there until the early 1990s, when the base was closed following the reunification of Germany and opening of borders to the east.

Totten served two years in the army before his discharge in March 1955.

Now, the Iron Curtain is long gone and Germany is a united country once again. In many respects, it owes its renewed prosperity to the U.S. troops that served there throughout the Cold War.

"Look at it today," Totten said. "Germany is more American than we are. I remember that year and a half in Germany more than a lot of other things. It was an experience."

JIMMY CARTER TRAINED AT NAVY NUCLEAR SITE

Published February 18, 2002

Of all the modern presidents, none has more direct ties to Saratoga County than Jimmy Carter. In 1952, he was one of the navy's rising young stars assigned to a new atomic submarine program founded by Admiral Hyman Rickover. The navy commissioned General Electric Co. in Schenectady to develop one of two prototype subs, called the USS *Sea Wolf*.

Carter trained noncommissioned officers, took graduate courses in reactor technology and nuclear physics at Union College and gained practical experience at Knolls Atomic Power Laboratory in West Milton. There, he and colleagues collaborated with GE employees in constructing a prototype atomic power plant with a huge steel sphere built for training purposes.

A mock nuclear sub, complete with console, was built at GE in Schenectady, where prospective crews could receive hands-on training and experience.

Carter, his wife, Rosalynn, and their three young children lived in an apartment on Duanesburg Road in Schenectady.

At this time, Carter's military future appeared to have no limits. He had graduated fifty-ninth in a class of 820 midshipmen from the U.S. Naval Academy in 1946 and became a full lieutenant on June 1, 1952. He was among the few officers who possessed the intellect, technical skills and engineering background needed to help lead America's fledgling atomic submarine program.

Then personal tragedy struck when his father, Earl, died from cancer at the Carter family home in Plains, Georgia. In early 1953, the future president had a difficult choice to make.

Earl Carter's peanut farm holdings totaled more than five thousand acres, and his business interests provided a livelihood for Plains's fifteen hundred residents. If Jimmy Carter didn't return home to manage things, the community might literally dry up and blow away.

Earl Carter had been a pillar of the community who positively influenced people throughout southwest Georgia. His son felt that he had to do the same.

Carter friend Bill Lalor said, "It was almost like a medieval idea, that one man was responsible for the souls in the town of Plains, Georgia… Without his father those people were not going to have any means to live… He [Jimmy] was just torn over the obligation to those people and the idea that he was picked to be chief engineer of the *Sea Wolf*."

However, Carter was also a bit disenchanted with military life and didn't relish the idea of constantly fighting for advancement with no place to call home.

Rosalynn Carter said that her husband "did not think he could ever do anything in his life to have an impact on people's lives like his father's life had made. I think he thought he could work in the navy...and not really make a difference to people."

Little did Carter realize that Plains would repay him by launching a political career that took him all the way to the White House. But Rosalynn Carter was dead-set against going back to Georgia. She was married to a man who would almost certainly become admiral one day. Instead, he was taking her back to a poor southern town with no library, no kindergarten and not even a swimming pool.

"She almost quit on me," Jimmy Carter said later.

However, he had undergone a fundamental change that helped account for this course of action.

Biographer Peter G. Bourne wrote, "The excitement the navy seemed to offer in his youth had been replaced, as he matured, with a more sober assessment of the true military purpose."

Carter reflected, "God did not intend for me to spend my life working on instruments of destruction to kill people."

One of his great achievements as president was brokering the Camp David peace accord between Israel and Egypt. Likewise, Carter has devoted much of his post-presidential life working to promote humanitarian and peacekeeping efforts at home and abroad.

Sources: Jimmy Carter *by Peter G. Bourne and* Jimmy Carter: The Man, The Myth *by Victor Lasky.*

WILTON MAN WORKED WITH CARTER

Bernard "Bunny" Doescher worked at Knolls Atomic Power Laboratory in West Milton at the same time as Jimmy Carter. Doescher, seventy-three, of Wilton, was a civilian employee and spent forty-one years there. Carter was a naval officer who worked roughly one year at Knolls before resigning from the military in October 1953 so that he could return home to Plains, Georgia, and take over his father's farming interests.

Doescher had almost daily contact with Carter during their time together. "He had such a brilliant mind," he recalled. "Very intelligent. Of all the presidents who graduated from service academies, Jimmy Carter had the highest scholastic average."

But Doescher never pegged Carter to become a politician, much less thirty-ninth president of the United States.

"He was very nice to talk to," Doescher said. "He never talked politics. He talked a lot about Georgia. He liked the Saratoga-Schenectady area, though."

Doescher said he can still picture Carter's wife, Rosalynn, picking him up at work each day.

"She used to wait for him outside the building," he said.

Doescher never learned why Carter left Knolls until years later. He lost all touch with Carter until 1976, when he heard the Democratic presidential candidate being interviewed on WGY talking about his early days living in Schenectady.

"I said, 'Oh boy, that's my Jimmy Carter!'" Doescher said with a laugh. "He was quite a man."

VIETNAM WAR

MAKING PEACE WITH THE PAST

Published May 1, 2009

Forty-one years ago, John Svandrlik was lying in a hospital bed after losing his leg in a noncombat injury while serving overseas in Vietnam. That summer of 1968 was among the most turbulent in American history, with the assassination of Robert F. Kennedy, riots at the Democratic National Convention and racial tensions boiling over from the death, in April, of the Reverend Dr. Martin Luther King Jr.

For Svandrlik, aside from his own personal loss, the hardest part was returning home and seeing Vietnam protestors chanting, "Hell no, we won't go!"

"It was frustrating, anger, knowing I still had comrades overseas," he said.

On Thursday (April 30, 2009), the thirty-fourth anniversary of the war's conclusion, Svandrlik led a ceremony dedicating a plaque to all Vietnam veterans at Gerald B.H. Solomon Saratoga National Cemetery's memorial path. He remembers exactly how he felt on April 30, 1975, when the last U.S. troops left Vietnam during the fall of Saigon.

"I was very happy to see the war over but was disappointed about the way it ended," Svandrlik said. "It was supposed to be peace with honor. I didn't see it that way."

He joined the navy in 1966 as a nineteen-year-old, two years out of high school.

"My father and uncle were veterans, and both of my grandfathers," the Fort Ann resident said. "It was something that was in the family—to serve."

Today, he's president of Vietnam Veterans of America, Adirondack Chapter 79, whose members include a number of Saratoga County residents.

Jim Brown of South Glens Falls joined the Marine Corps in 1965 for reasons similar to Svandrlik's. His father, James, was a marine night flight radar operator who served during World War II and was shot down and killed in Korea, four days after Jim's sixth birthday.

When the time came, Brown wanted to carry on his father's legacy of service. He spent twenty months in Vietnam doing aircraft maintenance at Chu Lai, a coastal city on the South China Sea, where the United States had a huge air base.

One of his worst and most memorable experiences came during the North Vietnamese Army's Tet Offensive in January 1968.

"The last rocket they fired that night hit the bomb depot," Brown said. "The concussion leveled our hangar. We knew they were coming, so we had taken shelter in a protective bunker."

Normally, he worked on planes during the day that took off on night missions.

"That night, instead of coming back to Chu Lai, they went to Thailand," he said. "Then they flew back to us in the morning. We worked on them and sent them back out. We never really stopped working. We improvised."

Saratoga Lake resident Steve Weinstein served two tours in Vietnam—April 1968 to April 1969 and February 1970 to February 1971—with the top-secret U.S. Army Security Agency. His covert unit intercepted and decoded North Vietnamese radio transmissions to track enemy troop movement and positions.

"I logged thirteen hundred hours doing airborne radio direction finding," the Bronx native said. "We flew in a twin-engine Beechcraft Bonanza—the pilot, copilot and me. If the NVA was on the move, weren't where they were supposed to be, we'd send in an air strike. Right after I got home, one of our planes was shot down. Five guys were lost. One of them sat next to me."

Understandably, many Vietnam vets would never go back there because of the memories of lost comrades and the suffering they endured. Weinstein, however, has made three return trips and is planning a fourth.

An avid ham radio operator, he introduced the hobby to Vietnam in 1998, when the Clinton administration opened up trade relations.

"It was very strange," he said, recalling the flight from Hong Kong to Saigon. "I sat next to a Vietnamese girl who was four years old when she left. Her parents were sending her back because her grandparents were getting old. She was very apprehensive. She didn't know how they were going to treat her."

Uneasy too, at first, Weinstein was pleasantly surprised by the reception he got, detecting no anti-American sentiment wherever he went. "The country is communist, but the people have a tremendous amount of freedom," he said. "Their young people don't want to know about the war. They want to be like Americans. I stood behind one guy who had three cellphones."

A year later, Weinstein took his wife along on a second ham radio–related trip and returned again in 2004 for sightseeing and tourism, mostly in the south. The nation is now the Socialist Republic of Vietnam.

At one point, he visited underground tunnels—virtual cities—that NVA soldiers lived in during the war.

"They used to sneak out at night to fight," Weinstein said. "Our guys, sent in to flush them out, were called tunnel rats."

Nearby, his Vietnamese guide—dressed in an NVA uniform—pointed out a large depression in the ground, now overgrown by jungle.

"It was a crater from a B-52 bomb," Weinstein said. "It was so big. I don't know how they lived."

Today, he communicates regularly with Vietnamese friends he's made through ham radio. Other acquaintances through the years run the gamut from Walter Cronkite—Weinstein installed an antenna in his Manhattan apartment—to the late King Hussein of Jordan.

"I met him personally," Weinstein said. "He loved ham radio. I had his card. It's a very unique hobby. It's a great way to learn about people. There's something about talking to someone ten thousand miles away without wires. Everyone thought the Internet would knock out 'hams.' The ham is holding its own."

For reasons he can't explain, Vietnam holds a special allure for Weinstein, drawing him back to explore every corner. In January, he wants to be there for the start of the lunar year called Tet.

"The whole country stops for ten days to celebrate," he said.

Like most veterans, he had his share of close calls and painful experiences. In April 1970, a Russian-made rocket hit barracks where he was stationed in Da Nang, killing three civilian avionics workers. During one of his nighttime intelligence flights, the plane detected radar lock from an enemy hand-held missile.

"We were flying near the DMZ [Demilitarized Zone]," Weinstein said. "The pilot went straight down from eleven thousand feet and leveled off over the South China Sea. I'm just glad I can talk about it and still remember."

And, like many Vietnam veterans, the sixty-one-year-old Weinstein deals with afflictions—seen and unseen—from his time overseas. During a reunion last year of his 509th Radio Research Group, fourteen of nineteen men reported having diabetes, a possible result of exposure to Agent Orange, which the United States used to defoliate jungles to reveal enemy locations.

"We all come from different parts of the country," he said. "It's all from service over there."

Svandrlik, while dedicating the new Vietnam veterans' monument, praised everyone who did their part.

"Those of us in attendance today know who the real heroes of this nation are," he said. "They lie under all the tombstones we passed on the way back here to this memorial path. This plaque is meant to show the visitors that come upon it that their service was not in vain."

WILTON SUPERVISOR ART JOHNSON REMEMBERS

Published June 9, 2006

Art Johnson didn't rush to see the Vietnam War Memorial when it first opened in Washington, D.C. He simply wasn't ready for the memories.

Having served in Southeast Asia, he knows all too well that his own name could have been among the thousands listed.

"It's very moving and very emotional," Johnson said of his first visit to the memorial. "A lot came back, but a lot of names are on that wall, too."

He's one of three Vietnam veterans on Saratoga County's board of supervisors, along with Milton's Frank Thompson and Greenfield's Al Janik, who will be leading ceremonies at the Moving Wall this week at Shenantaha Creek Park in Malta.

The original Vietnam War Memorial, built in 1982, played a major role in healing a nation's wounds following one of the most divisive times in American history.

"I'm glad that eventually people came around and started to recognize that Vietnam War vets were not treated the same as other veterans," Johnson said.

At the same time, he knows what it's like to come home and be greeted by derision and scorn rather than flags, banners and parades. An Albany native, Johnson was drafted in October 1966 and spent a year overseas beginning in early 1967. His maintenance unit was attached to the First Cavalry at Ahn Ke in the central highlands.

"I don't know why they tried to make me a mechanic," he said, laughing.

With an accountant's background, he simply wasn't cut out to work on two-and-a-half-ton trucks, jeeps and howitzers. He was among the fortunate ones who escaped infantry duty, but he faced his share of danger just the same.

"There were always incoming mortar rounds," Johnson said. "You really didn't know who your enemy was. It was just not an easy war to win. It was always going to be a ground fight. There was no end in sight."

But in some ways, coming home was even harder.

"After I did get back, to see the protesters, it was kind of disturbing," he said. "After all the sacrifices you went through, there was no one to welcome you home, and people really looked down on you. I think young people today look up to the military, and the Iraq veterans will not have the same experience as Vietnam vets. They'll come back as heroes."

Johnson dealt with his reception the best way he knew how.

"I was proud to be a veteran, but I didn't get on the other side of the protesters," he said. "I came back, I got a job and life goes on. You put it behind you. I was so grateful just to come home, I didn't dwell on it."

After he landed a job as a state tax auditor, Johnson and his wife, Sandy, moved to Wilton in the early 1970s. Eventually, he became a presiding officer, charged with settling tax cases, and became active in public service.

Johnson's office has numerous glossy color photos showing him with celebrities and political comrades. Just inside the doorway, there's a small one, in black and white. All it shows is a finger pointing to a name on the Vietnam memorial, which Johnson has since been to several times.

"The first and even the second time was certainly the hardest for me," he said. "Your name could have been one of the thousands on the wall."

VETS VISIT THE WALL

Published June 10, 2006

Thousands turned up from throughout the region to pay respects to friends and loved ones whose names are on the Moving Wall during its second day in the area.

"I lost a best friend, Nelson McKenna," said Ted Howley of Queensbury. "We all signed up together. Medically I didn't make it—kidneys. I felt bad all these years that I didn't go with him, and he didn't come back. Every time his name's brought up, every time I go by his house or see places we used to hang out, I think about him."

McKenna's name is among the more than fifty-eight thousand on the 250-foot-long memorial, one of two half-size replicas of the Vietnam Memorial in Washington, D.C., that tour the nation each year.

"We used to call him 'Monks,'" Howley said, chuckling. "He used to be able to climb the highest trees we could find. I could describe this guy right down to how much he weighed."

For Howley and countless others, the wall is serving its intended purpose of helping people come to grips with long-held grief and emotions.

"It's a good thing they're doing here," he said. "Hopefully it'll make people feel better about what's going on today."

Francis R. Bessette of Saratoga Springs was in Vietnam from 1966 to 1967.

"I'm wondering how many of these guys who got killed didn't want to go over there but did because they were asked to," he said.

Hal Bigelow, fifty-three, of Quaker Springs, considers himself among the lucky ones who didn't get taken in the draft. His birthday is October 10 (10/10), the tenth date that came up, but the draft was a two-phase process. Once birth dates were drawn, all numbers were put back in and drawn again. This time, he came up number 312, well beyond the cut-off for selection.

"I'll never forget it," he said. "It was an extra layer of randomness. If it was based on birth dates alone, I would have had to go."

Bigelow and his wife, Marian, are among the many volunteers helping visitors find names on the wall this weekend.

"I just wanted to do a little bit to honor those who served," he said.

His wife added, "Personally, I was against the war, but I was never against the service people. This has nothing to do with whether you were for or against the war. This is to honor the people who served."

The names of soldiers missing in action are identified with symbols different from those confirmed dead.

"It's real sad," said Jacob Holmes of Gloversville. "I can imagine the dramatic pain the relatives go through. For years and years, you don't know if they're dead or not."

Many people held white slips of paper to the wall and tried to etch the engraved names with black markers.

"When they said it was here, I had to come," said Indian Lake resident Bill Stewart, fifty-seven, an air force veteran. "I was at the wall in Washington when they dedicated it."

Stewart was an aircraft mechanic stationed in Korea but also saw time in Vietnam.

"We were in the tactical air command, on twenty-four-hour mobile alert," he said. "We used to go all over Southeast Asia."

Stewart started talking about a good friend who had gotten married and was killed in action less than a year later. Then he couldn't say any more.

Mechanicville native David Amoroso looked at the memorial from a distance as people slowly made their way along the red-carpeted walkway in front of it. He spent three years, eight months and twenty-seven days in the navy in the early 1960s.

"Everybody was sweating the same thing: are you going to go to school, aboard ship or Vietnam?" he said.

I went through boot camp with a guy. I went to the Caribbean, and he went in the medics. When I came home on leave after the cruise, I was sitting on the stoop reading the newspaper, and there was his picture. He had gotten killed in Vietnam. I'll never forget it. That left an impact on me about how lucky I was. I was only nineteen years old when that happened.

JEFF CLARK: GUNG-HO FOR AMERICA

Published July 4, 2008

From combat helicopter missions over Vietnam to top-secret European spy flights, Jeff Clark knows what it means to put his life on the line.

He didn't, however, always have the support of a grateful nation. Forty years ago, when he joined the army, the United States was more divided than at any time since the Civil War, and protesters, including Clark's brother, demonstrated against the war in Southeast Asia.

Four decades later, as he reflects about Independence Day, America's young people are all the evidence Clark needs that the United States was and always will be a beacon of hope for freedom-loving people around the world.

"I think they're kind of like the new greatest generation," he said.

You've seen pictures of American GIs giving candy to little kids during World War II. Today, in Iraq, the GIs love kids just as much. Now they're giving them soccer balls. Sometimes we take this country for granted. Whether it's providing money for AIDS research in Africa or community service and charities here at home, it's just a marvelous, marvelous country with some of the best people on Earth.

Next to his own family, the fate of American troops is still most near and dear to his heart, especially those in the army's First Infantry Division, the legendary "Big Red 1," that he served with in Vietnam.

"I keep track of the division and keep track of what's going on," he said.

I was extremely fortunate to be in the First Division. It was a very significant part of my life. It has such a storied history. In World War I, under the command of General "Black Jack" Pershing, it was the first expeditionary field force, the first unit in France. There's a famous quote, "Lafayette, we are here!" It was an extremely proud division with a lot of esprit de corps.

That enthusiasm also carried the division through World War II and kept it going in Vietnam, where many U.S. soldiers had huge morale problems, unsure who or what they were fighting against, which Clark blames on political leadership at the time.

"All wars have mistakes," he said.

The best-laid and well-intentioned plans go awry. [In Vietnam] *we should have used the strategy that General Petraeus has so successfully implemented in Iraq, having our troops live with the people, not only protecting them from the fascist terrorists, but providing civic action projects—building schools, water and waste plants and generally improving the quality of their lives— and partnering with the Iraqis on their regional security.*

It's clearly not enough to take on the oppressors as we did in Vietnam. In that case, much the same was happening as in Iraq of 2005 to 2007. The Viet Cong would terrorize a village, slaughtering their leaders in a gruesome way and rendering their populace impotent to rise up against them, creating a de facto force against the government and the U.S.

People he fought side by side with were among the fifty-eight thousand U.S. soldiers who made the ultimate sacrifice. Clark's first tour was from 1969 to 1970 flying a Huey helicopter on all kinds of missions—from delivering goods and supplies to literally sniffing out the enemy with high-tech devices that could detect high concentrations of ammonia from the sweat of soldiers in the hot, steamy jungles.

"Fifty percent of our flights were night gunship missions," he said. "Our mission was to find trouble and engage."

Most of the time, this meant flying just one hundred feet off the ground at fifteen knots, making him extremely vulnerable to hostile fire. In one harrowing experience, his chopper took on an entire company of enemy combatants to save a U.S. boat tied up along a river.

"For one split second, I totally believed that everyone in the world was shooting at me," Clark said. "I was never wounded, but the helicopter took quite a few hits. It's aluminum. When bullets hit, it makes the sound of a steel Zippo being dropped on the floor."

He came home after a year, learned how to fly airplanes and went back in 1972 for another full year's duty. He was fortunately spared the danger of further combat situations. As the Vietnam War wound down, the second phase of Clark's military career was just beginning to unfold. He spent four years flying some of the most sophisticated aircraft ever built, such as the OV-1 Mohawk, whose side-looking radar kept track of Soviet tank movements near the border of East Germany.

This brought regular encounters with Soviet MiG fighters.

"Sometimes they'd come right for you and break off," he said. "They'd never cross the border."

And sometimes, like a scene from the movie *Top Gun*, they'd engage missile lock on Clark's plane—just to give him a scare.

"That's not a good feeling," he said, smiling.

The last six years of his service time were spent flying VIPs, from ambassadors to four-star generals, to all parts of the globe. After a quarter century in the army, he switched gears and began flying for Pan American Airlines but gave it up after just five months.

"I found that flying for an airline was a lot less exciting," he said.

Next came a stint as aviation safety manager for Johnson Controls, which had a defense contract in the Marshall Islands, where rocket scientists were doing Star Wars missile shield research. However, Clark, a Ticonderoga native, and his wife, Laura, began yearning for upstate New York, and a travel magazine article about Saratoga Springs was all the encouragement they needed.

Today, he runs a local Ameriprise Financial Services franchise at the Collamer Building on Broadway in Saratoga Springs. With three grown daughters and two granddaughters, the Clarks are both quite active in the community, still giving back in a variety of ways. He is a 2001 Leadership Saratoga graduate and a former local magistrate, spent six years on the Brookside Museum board and is a current Downtown Business Association board member. He also loves kayaking, while Laura, a children's librarian at Saratoga Springs Public Library, is an ultra-marathoner.

"Every once in a while I have a yen to get back in the cockpit, but life is kind of busy right now," Clark said.

Whether it's coordinating local running and snowshoe events or managing his office, his flight career continues to pay dividends.

"Planning is crucial," he said. "Planning and preparation. Without that, the results can be severe."

During his military service, Clark was awarded forty-eight air medals, including one with a "V" for valor, a Distinguished Flying Cross, two Bronze Stars and a Legion of Merit. His greatest reward was simply serving alongside America's finest young men and women and knowing that future generations will pick up where he left off.

"It just makes you appreciate this country so much more," he said. "It's truly remarkable."

BOB NEVINS: HELICOPTER PILOT

Published November 10, 2008

In the fleeting seconds it took his helicopter to hit the jungle floor, Bob Nevins got a crash course in survival that's lasted a lifetime.

While attempting to rescue wounded American GIs in Vietnam, his unarmed medevac chopper was hit by a rocket-propelled grenade that instantly killed two of his four crewmates and sent the machine plummeting 150 feet into an exploding fireball, from which he somehow miraculously escaped.

Nevins spent the next twenty years, like many veterans, trying to understand his fate—why he's been able to enjoy life's rich blessings while losing so many close friends who made the ultimate sacrifice at such a young age.

"That's what takes away the thrill of victory," said this highly decorated Vietnam vet. "You either have to leave it behind and let it go or you get stuck in the past. You have to come to terms with it."

In a year's time, from July 4, 1970, to the same date in 1971, Nevins flew more than five hundred missions over South Vietnam.

"As a twenty-one-year-old kid dodging bullets, you don't have time to analyze what's going on," he said. "You're just trying to stay alive. It was like being a firefighter going into the World Trade Center, every other day."

An army chief warrant officer, Nevins, now fifty-nine, came home with a Purple Heart, a Soldier's Medal and three Distinguished Flying Crosses and was considered for the Congressional Medal of Honor. Vietnam vets, however, weren't treated like the heroes of 9/11 and most other wars.

Helicopter pilot Bob Nevins was shot down over Vietnam on January 15, 1971.

"You got criticized after you came out," he said. "All that and fifty cents would have got me a cup of coffee when I came home. Things have changed a lot since then."

His 326th Medical Battalion, flying Huey helicopters, saved countless American lives while venturing into hostile territory against an unseen enemy day and night. Rules of international warfare forbid them from being armed, and as a medical team, they weren't supposed to be fired on, but deep in the Southeast Asian jungle, the Viet Cong didn't care about rules.

Nevins's brush with death came on January 15, 1971, about six months into his overseas deployment. A call came in that U.S. soldiers out on patrol had been seriously wounded.

"There were booby traps everywhere," he said.

Flying to the scene, his helicopter hovered over the jungle canopy, trying to extricate victims with a penetrator—a cable that would hoist soldiers to safety. On most occasions, a Cobra gunship would accompany medevac choppers, but this time there wasn't one immediately available.

The Viet Cong often tried to shoot down medical helicopters, which they hoped would kill its crew and fall on American soldiers below as well. The attack happened so quickly that there was no time to react. Yet Nevins recalls everything moving in slow motion as his life flashed before his eyes.

On impact, the grenade blew his crew chief out the door, and a medic was also killed instantly. Shrapnel struck the pilot, and the chopper began making an inverted dive. At the same time, a fireball ripped through the cockpit, sucking the air out of Nevins's lungs.

"We set the jungle on fire," he said. "I opened my eyes and was kind of wondering why I'm not dead."

Fortunately, the accident broke a hole in the bottom of the chopper that allowed him to get out, but two of his comrades—a second medic and the pilot—were still trapped inside. The medic had an exposed kidney and a hole the size of a fist in his back. Nevins, however, got him to safety and was able to locate the ground patrol's sergeant, whose own men were wounded, including a double amputee.

"We could hear the VC crunching through the bushes behind," he said.

Radioing for help, within fifteen minutes four gunships showed up and began firing everything they had, giving Nevins the cover he needed to go back and extricate the pilot, who was still inside the burning chopper. A pair of navy Phantoms and an Australian bomber also showed up to help the cause.

The scene continued to unfold as another medevac chopper arrived. Still surrounded by the enemy, Nevins carried and half dragged his wounded crewmates so they could be lifted to safety. In the process, he saw the double amputee, who was conscious and lying on the ground.

"He gave me a thumbs-up," he said, the scene a permanent fixture in his mind.

Finally, with help from two more medical helicopters, the entire group was taken out of harm's way. Suffering from extensive burns, cuts and abrasions over most of his body, Nevins spent the next several weeks recuperating and could have had a one-way ticket home.

But he stayed to fly again.

"These guys just all did this for me, and I'm there to do that for them," he said. "I felt so bonded to these people. You felt you were obligated to stay there and protect them. This was routine stuff in Vietnam. There's no war heroes over there. This was the norm."

Soon after, steps were put in motion for him to receive the Medal of Honor. However, because he was flying a medical mission, the incident technically wasn't combat, and he got the Soldier's Medal instead. The award was personally bestowed on him by General Sidney Berry, commanding general of the 101st Airborne, who later became superintendent at West Point. By definition, the medal is awarded to any person of the U.S. Armed Forces who, while serving in any capacity with the U.S. Army, "distinguishes himself or herself by heroism not involving actual conflict with an enemy."

Nevins smiles ruefully at the thought of it but doesn't complain, realizing full well that many Medals of Honor are awarded posthumously.

"The price you pay far exceeds any reward you get for it," he said.

Coming back home, armed with incredible firsthand experience, he began fighting another battle—for the establishment of a civilian air ambulance corps. This time, the enemy was human nature, because everyone he approached showed no interest or gave all-too-familiar responses:

"What's in it for me?"

"How much will it cost?

"We don't do it that way."

Nevins knew, however, that U.S. soldiers who had been shot in Vietnam stood a better chance of survival than car crash victims on American highways because army helicopters could whisk GIs to hospitals much faster than ambulance vehicles back home. He spent years trying to show the value of transporting trauma patients by helicopter and formed his own company, Eastern Medevac.

Unfortunately, it never got off the ground.

"I was met with resistance all the way," he said. "I was ten years ahead of my time. Now they're everywhere throughout the country, so I accomplished my mission. It doesn't matter who gets the credit."

He did, however, get some long-overdue recognition when, on October 26, 1977, the nonprofit group No Greater Love named him an Outstanding Vietnam-Era Veteran. Other recipients included former Dallas Cowboys Hall of Fame quarterback Roger Staubach. Nevins got to meet President Jimmy Carter and was honored during ceremonies at the Kennedy Center in Washington, D.C.

Later, still in love with aviation, he became a commercial airline pilot and has been flying for American Eagle, a division of American Airlines, for more than twenty years. On the morning of September 11, 2001, his plane bound for Toronto was the last one to leave the ground at Boston's Logan International Airport.

He was in flight, right over Saratoga County, when he got word that a plane had struck the World Trade Center. The next five days were gut wrenching—he was separated from his wife, Andrea, and their two sons—before he was allowed to return home from Canada.

In some respects, Vietnam is a distant memory, but the lessons learned there provide constant daily reminders about the value of life and its fragility.

"Now I'm taking it easy, sipping coffee at thirty thousand feet," Nevins said, smiling.

An avid horse racing fan, he's made friends with numerous high-profile jockeys and trainers and might partner with a friend to start his own stable.

"That's what I want to do for the next twenty years," he said. "It's the biggest adrenaline rush you can get without getting shot at."

WAR ON TERROR

TOM BROKAW INTERVIEWS COMPANY C

Published April 16, 2005

Tom Brokaw covered civil rights, Watergate and the end of the Cold War during his years with NBC, many of them as anchor of the NBC Nightly News. America's war on terrorism will probably be the most important story of the early twenty-first century, he said during a visit to Saratoga Springs. Brokaw was in town to interview local national guardsmen for an upcoming NBC *Dateline* documentary called *To War and Back*.

Brokaw interviewed members of Company C (Charlie Company), who joined the New York Army National Guard in Glens Falls. The program focuses on soldiers' experiences in Iraq, their challenges upon returning home and the similarities they share with veterans of other wars. Brokaw interviewed soldiers at the Saratoga Diner on South Broadway and visited other Saratoga Springs sites such as Congress Park. After filming at the diner, he interviewed more soldiers at the Bullpen bar on Caroline Street.

Company C spent ten months in Iraq before returning home in January 2005. It saw considerable action and was based mostly in Samarra. That's where Private First Class Nathan Brown of South Glens Falls was killed in action on Easter Sunday 2004. NBC crews were present when Brown's family held a remembrance ceremony at his grave at the Gerald B.H. Solomon Saratoga National Cemetery.

The war in Iraq marks the first time since World War II that New York Army National Guard members have seen combat. Specialist Rob Hemsing

Newsman Tom Brokaw spent several days in Saratoga Springs, in April 2005, interviewing army national guardsmen for an NBC *Dateline* documentary, *To War and Back*.

of Glens Falls was wounded during the attack that killed Brown, and Chad Byrne of Hudson Falls was also involved. In addition, Brokaw interviewed Sergeant Ken Comstock of Ballston Spa, who was badly injured in a separate incident. (*To War and Back* aired in December 2005.)

Brokaw is also well known for authoring *The Greatest Generation*, a series of stories about men and women who came of age during the Great Depression and defended their country in World War II. He autographed copies of his book for fans and well-wishers who turned out to see him during his brief stay in Saratoga Springs.

While here, he also took time out to discuss his experiences with veterans of all generations. When asked what impressed him most about the national guardsmen he interviewed, he responded:

> *People always ask me what are the most memorable interviews I've ever done. They expect me to say Gorbachev or Dr. King or the presidents. Actually, these are the interviews that linger with me—all over the world,*

ordinary people who do exceptional things and then don't expect to get any attention. That's the real story of humanity.

By the time people get to the top, they're pretty practiced in how they respond to you, and they're kind of on autopilot. When you're with these young men who have been in Iraq, they joined the National Guard thinking it would maybe help them get to college and then finding themselves in harm's way and serving their country, that's the real fabric of the country. That's what you tend to remember.

He noted similarities between Iraq war veterans and those from the greatest generation.

For one thing, when they get in combat, it's about saving a buddy. They quickly forget about why they joined. It's really about survival and protecting each other. The bonds that are formed in uniform stay forever for most of them. There's this quiet pride in what they're doing and why they're doing it.

I always believe that the best of American life is found in places like this. That's what holds us together. It's not at the extremes. It's really in the heartland, and the heartland is everywhere. The people who went to World War II and came home didn't stop giving back to their country, and these kids won't either.

Brokaw notes that there are some things these young soldiers don't want to discuss.

A lot of times, it's hard for them to talk about it. These kids have said that they haven't told their families or friends everything they saw because it's both too difficult for them to remember it and they didn't want to put their families through that. That's not unusual.

One of the World War II guys that I interviewed said that when he goes into a bar and people are talking about combat he walks out, in part because he said people talking about it haven't been there. I think you'll find the same thing here.

He said that Charlie Company was chosen for this documentary because "its emblematic."

First of all, this is a war in which the guard and the reserves have had a very substantial role. They're volunteers, they're not drafted. They joined the guard for reasons other than going into combat, and they got beat up, and they came home and they're trying to find their lives in the midst of a country that is both paying attention to the war in Iraq but not being asked to sacrifice in the same way that they were during World War II.

So there's a kind of a disconnect between people in uniform and those of us in civilian life.

Brokaw admitted that it's difficult for him to interview families of fallen American heroes such as Nathan Brown of South Glens Falls.

Every situation where somebody loses somebody in war, it's an especially poignant loss because that young man died on behalf of all of us. So we all have a claim on his life. That makes it always harder.

There are generally within the families conflicting emotions. There's enormous pride, a great sense of grief, often anger about what's going on. What's reassuring to his mother and to his family, I'm sure, is the kind of continuing bonds that these young men feel with him...their determination to make sure that what he stood for stays alive.

That's part of the reason we're here.

NATE BROWN: KILLED IN IRAQ, EASTER 2004

Published April 16, 2006

Rick Brown visits his son's grave site at the Gerald B.H. Solomon Saratoga National Cemetery two or three times per month. Sometimes, he doesn't know why. He just ends up there.

Brown, his wife, Kathy, and their daughter, Vickie, went there on Tuesday with a purpose—to mark the second anniversary of Private First Class Nathan P. Brown's death while serving in the U.S. Army National Guard in Iraq.

"There's so much that he's missing," Rick Brown said. "I usually don't like coming here, but it's always a good thing. I always feel better when I leave."

About a dozen soldiers, some veterans and some still in active duty, joined the Browns, who live in Glens Falls. There was no formal ceremony, no speech, no start and no end.

Nathan Brown's headstone is the first in a long row of gray granite markers.

"He always wanted to be an individualist," Rick Brown said. "There's so many things that he used to do. He was the type of kid, he could bounce off

Private First Class Nathan Brown's mother, Kathy, and sister, Vickie, visit his grave at Gerald B.H. Solomon Saratoga National Cemetery.

the porch and do a handstand riding down the street on a bicycle. He was just so full of life and energy."

His fourteen-year-old sister said:

> *Every once in a while, when I look at my Aunt Carrie's house, the one we used to live in when he was with us, I can actually still see him jumping off the front porch. I love him and I miss him. Without him, it feels like there's nothing left to have fun for, I guess. But I do anyway because I have my friends.*

Scenery surrounding the national cemetery is peaceful and serene.

It's sacred, hallowed ground, but at the same time, it's full of energy, like Nathan Brown was, because the earth is coming back to life following another long winter. Red buds cap the tops of maple trees, brown grass is giving way to green and in a neighboring farm field, a tractor tills the ground in anticipation of spring planting.

Nathan Brown couldn't be there, not in person, but he's just as much a part of his family and loved ones as he was the day he left home.

"He's in heaven, so he doesn't feel alone," his father said. "Now, his grandma's [Beatrice Ryan] with him. She passed away on the first [April

1]. He doesn't feel alone, for sure, because Grammy was a big part of his life."

Kathy Brown, however, is concerned about the general public's attitude toward U.S. soldiers serving in Iraq and elsewhere abroad.

"I think that we're slacking in forgetting about our soldiers over there and the ones coming home," she said.

> *I think the community is starting to get comfortable again, and I'm afraid it's just another time before we have another local soldier that's going to fall. We need to stay on our toes and remember these guys. We need to be more compassionate, more caring and let them know that just because everyone doesn't think the war is just, what they're doing is.*

Yellow ribbons are an important visible show of support, but there are more practical ways to let soldiers know that their country is behind them, Kathy Brown said.

"Packages, cards, help their families," she said.

> *That's a big thing. A lot of these guys go over there, I think, worried about their families. Their family's hot water tank or furnace might go. They might need a little help. I think the guys take a lot of comfort, and it makes their job easier, knowing that they're being taken care of.*

Roy Pechtel, whose son, Ryan, served with Nathan Brown, was among those who turned out for Tuesday's memorial.

"My heart goes out to those people right there," he said, as the Browns walked among the grave sites. "If I didn't learn anything else about war, I learned how easy it is to cry, because you never know."

His son has been home since December 31, 2004, and is still going about the long, arduous process of getting on with his life.

"It's getting better every day," Roy Pechtel said. "When he first got home, naturally, everybody had their problems and that. He's doing good. They just need people there to listen to them when they do want to talk. As a parent, that's basically what we do. We don't ask questions. We just wait for them to open up."

For several months after his son came home, Roy Pechtel stayed active collecting truckloads of donations for U.S. soldiers overseas.

"Even though it's not my son over there, it's somebody else's son or daughter," he said.

He's since handed the baton off to other folks who are keeping up the effort, but like Kathy Brown, he's concerned that people are forgetting. As support for the war has waned, it's possible that soldiers are getting shortchanged in the process.

"You take the mom of a fallen soldier protesting," Kathy Brown said. "I can understand her grief. I know how bad she hurts. But now, it's getting a little dishonoring, not only to her son but all the fallen, the disabled, everybody, all our soldiers. Yes, I want them home, I want them all home, but that's not possible right now. So do something to help them."

JIM PABIS: CITIZEN-SOLDIER

Published November 11, 2007

Jim Pabis didn't envision himself taking cover from mortar fire and a hailstorm of bullets seventeen years ago. His first decade in the service was

Lieutenant Colonel Jim Pabis commanded a New York military police detachment that helped manage twenty-three thousand detainees held by coalition forces in Iraq.

spent on routine training duties, teaching West Point cadets and improving his own military skills.

Then 9/11 hit, and his job became much more serious, providing security for metropolitan New York transportation hubs—tunnels, bridges, rail lines and airports. Nothing, however, prepared him for last year's phone call when this citizen-soldier learned he was going to Iraq.

"I was literally driving down Route 490 in Rochester," said Pabis, who at thirty-eight is one of the National Guard's youngest lieutenant colonels. "I was out doing my annual training at our home station, which is kind of nice. You're doing administrative stuff, improvements in the armory."

A few months later, he stepped off a military transport plane in Baghdad and was hit square in the face with 120-degree desert temperatures that could be likened to a blast from a giant hair dryer.

That was August 2006. A year later, he returned home with a Bronze Star, mixed emotions about U.S. involvement in Iraq and hard-won combat-environment experience.

Pabis, of Ballston Lake, commanded a New York military police detachment that helped manage the twenty-three thousand detainees held by coalition forces in Iraq. Those in custody had been identified as security threats, either because of overt hostile action or suspected involvement with insurgent or terrorist groups.

"Some of them clearly fall into the category of the most dangerous people in the world," Pabis said. "It's communal living, they're loose in there like cattle, and there's a challenge inherent in that. They can permeate each other; they can teach each other. So there's an issue of it becoming a training ground for terrorism."

As in many prisons, there are fights, riots and even murders within the inmate ranks. Unlike maximum-security state and federal facilities, where there's a great deal of prisoner control, the Iraqi sites are extremely difficult to monitor.

"These are wide open," Pabis said. "Some of the compounds have over one thousand folks in them, and some of them are bad dudes. They brutalize each other. When they kill somebody, they take their eyes out, they chop their hands off."

His unit didn't have combat missions, but the prison is still exposed to enemy attack. "We did take mortars. We did take rockets and we did take small arms fire," Pabis said.

There were periods when it would come every day, and then it would subside. We had a rocket that came within 150 meters, so it was close.

Small arms? I mean I've been under a car for twenty to twenty-five minutes. Ping! Ping! It sounds like a drill. You couldn't see them, but it appeared as though they had eyes on us. The safest zone is supposedly the Green Zone, and it gets indirect fire almost every day.

The toughest assignments involved transporting detainees to medical or court dates, outside the relative protection of prison surroundings, Pabis said.

"I went out more than I would have cared to. When you're driving on the streets, you're just holding onto your hat, and there's nothing you can do. You drive by a car parked on the side of the road and you hope it doesn't go off," recalled Pabis, grimacing with his eyes closed, as if holding his breath.

"The same thing with flying. They were shooting helicopters down for a while. So when you're up there, you're just waiting to see a rocket coming at you. It's a bit nerve-wracking."

Military service runs deep in the Pabis family. His father, Bill, was in the army during the height of the Cold War in the early 1960s, and Pabis's brother, Bill Jr., served in the Gulf War. In part, he wanted to continue the family's legacy, but ROTC also gave him the chance to get a college education. An Amsterdam native, Pabis went to Bishop Scully High School and then Northeastern University, where he came out a second lieutenant with a degree in criminal justice.

He's since earned an MBA while receiving all kinds of in-depth military training, from engineering to leadership skills, and was among a short list of officers chosen to instruct West Point cadets in the finer points of military science. He was put to the ultimate test when he was deployed to Iraq—the toughest classroom of all.

"For me, it was an opportunity to put into practice what I've been preaching all these years," he said. "You go to all these schools, both in the military and in business. Over there is just a true test of leadership principles under extremely stressful conditions. I was blessed with a great group of folks, and they really made it easy," he said.

Pabis has almost three and a half years left in his military commitment. His goal is to make colonel, reach twenty years and then decide whether to re-up.

"The biggest plus is I love the people that I've met all along the way, from second lieutenant until now," he said. "I'm grateful that I've experienced them, and I'm honored to have worked with them. And it's my little contribution to this great country we live in. I always wanted to be there if the call came."

His sacrifice while serving in Iraq wasn't just one of time, safety and effort. Like every soldier, his personal and professional life also was put on hold. Pabis owns Saratoga Resource, an executive recruiting firm in Saratoga Springs that finds prospects for corporate clients.

"I started and built the business from nothing in 1998 and had it humming along nicely," he said.

In fact, we had our best year in 2006. So it was just awful to leave that momentum. In addition, I'm the type of person that doesn't like asking anyone for anything, and in this case I had no options. Bill Canty, a local businessman and great friend, rose to the challenge and now has the business running better than when I left. I'm very grateful that it's at the level it is. I could have come back to nothing.

The toughest part, however, was leaving his girlfriend of two years, Sandy Hutchinson, his parents and other loved ones behind, knowing what they'd have to endure, not knowing from day to day whether he was safe. Fortunately, they were able to communicate with e-mail and periodic phone calls.

"It was a shock to our routine, but I must say, Sandy handled this like a trouper and supported me throughout the year," Pabis said.

Other commitments took a backseat to his military duty, also. He was Saratoga County Chamber of Commerce board chairman in 2005 and still on its board when his overseas duty began. He is on the Wesley Health Care Foundation, Unlimited Potential and Saratoga National Bank Community Advisory boards.

Some people might view the interruption as a setback, but Pabis sees it as a stepping-stone to stronger relationships and even more community involvement. "Getting back to it, I intend to make the overall picture better through this experience," he said.

While working and sometimes fighting overseas, he was aware that the American public isn't fully behind the war because modern technology, such as the Internet, keeps service people in touch with news around the globe.

"One of the things that make our country great is that people have the ability to question things like that," he said. "Our process, our system, the way we operate in the big picture is exactly what makes this country great."

Pabis said that U.S. troops do feel support from the e-mail, packages and phone calls from people back home. But when he returned to the Spa City this summer, it was difficult to watch people partying it up with little apparent regard for what's going on elsewhere in the world.

"I do get the impression that a lot of folks have no idea that it's even going on anymore," he said. "I feel for the guys who are still over there, and I think about them and I pray for them. I wish I could have brought them all home. I can't wait until they are."

For the record, he has no desire to go back.

"Once is enough," Pabis said.

CAROL HOTALING: "YELLOW RIBBON LADY"

Published October 21, 2009

Saratoga County's "Yellow Ribbon Lady" has won the National Guard Community Purple Award in recognition of her outstanding efforts on behalf of troops overseas.

Since Desert Storm, in the early 1990s, Carol Hotaling of Ballston Spa has made literally thousands of yellow ribbons to remind people of the sacrifice young men and women are making for their country, most recently in Iraq and Afghanistan.

Carol Hotaling, Saratoga County's "Yellow Ribbon Lady," has made countless decorations to remember U.S. troops overseas since the early 1990s.

"This is a national award; I'm very proud," said Hotaling, a Halfmoon native who went to school at Shenendehowa.

The National Guard Volunteer Award Recognition System, created in 2008, is designed to promote and recognize outstanding contributions made by individual volunteers and organizations. Recipients were presented with awards in four categories at the National Guard Volunteer and Youth Symposium in Dearborn, Michigan, in July.

Hotaling, who is limited in her ability to travel, could not attend. Instead, she was recognized recently during ceremonies at the Holiday Inn in Saratoga Springs. The award was presented by New York State Army National Guard lieutenant colonel Kelly Hilland and Brigadier General Patrick Murphy.

Hotaling was selected for the Community Purple Award based on her contributions and commitment to National Guard members and families. The award is presented to an individual, community group or faith-based organization that best exemplifies the true meaning of the "purple" concept by working with both air and army guard activities.

At airports, Hotaling has gone out of her way to present yellow ribbons to returning servicemen and women coming home from overseas duty. She has made literally tens of thousands of ribbons for funerals, memorial events, homecomings, reintegration events and parades.

One of her proudest accomplishments was establishing a Yellow Ribbon Day on April 9 of each year. The event was organized to remember Matt Maupin, the first prisoner of war captured in Iraq, in 2004, and other U.S. service members overseas. Locally, Yellow Ribbon Day is observed at Saratoga-Wilton Elks Club, and the annual event has become statewide, officially recognized by the governor's office.

"It's to remember all our troops," Hotaling said. "I'll never forget them."

AFGHANISTAN: A BATTLE FOR PEOPLE'S HEARTS

Published November 11, 2008

Local soldiers stationed in Afghanistan know when they're making progress by the smiles on children's faces. In a nation of abject poverty, where running water and electricity are quite often nonexistent, the U.S. military is winning over the hearts and minds of Afghan villagers by providing things necessary to their basic survival.

Saratoga County residents can join the fight against terrorism by providing much-needed ammunition such as teddy bears, winter clothing and school supplies.

"These people have so little," said Lieutenant Jared Jensen of Ballston Spa, who is scheduled to return home in December, following nine months of overseas duty.

Sergeant William Utermark of Saratoga Springs is due back in America this month.

"That's going to be the biggest thing I take back with me, how poor the country is and how much we take for granted in the States," he said.

Next to family and loved ones, there's one thing he's looking forward to most. "A big, ice-cold glass of milk," he said.

For Afghans, such things are almost impossible to come by, and when they are available, most people can't afford them. Yet it's not uncommon to find someone sharing a simple sandwich with three or four others.

"They're really some of the most generous people I've ever seen," said twenty-two-year-old Private First Class John Gallup of Mechanicville. "Being here makes you appreciate little things like clean running water. A majority of people don't even have that."

A 2004 Stillwater High School graduate, he's been in Afghanistan since mid-March and hopes to be home in early January. His service has been a sacrifice, but one he's made willingly.

"It's hard not being able to do simple things like get in a car and go someplace with friends," he said. "You miss your freedom, basically. But September 11 [2001] was a big deal for me. I joined the National Guard in late 2006. I just felt like I should serve my country and that being here in Afghanistan was the right thing to do."

U.S. troops routinely go out on two types of missions—military and humanitarian.

"We use humanitarian donations to assist us in our mission to train and mentor the Afghan security forces as they try to help their own communities," Lieutenant Colonel Paul Fanning of Malta said.

The poverty here is difficult if not impossible to comprehend. The simplest of items are eagerly welcomed by the people. While many people back home want to send care packages to the troops, the bottom line is we have more stuff than we need and sending school supplies to donate to Afghan children actually helps us with our mission.

At one time, villagers might have turned and headed indoors when they saw Americans coming, fearing reprisal from a deeply entrenched terrorist element. More and more, however, local U.S. soldiers say that they're welcomed with waves and friendly greetings.

"When most people trust government forces more than the Taliban or Al Qaeda, that's when we can say we've had success in this theatre," Jensen said.

Recently, an Afghan boys' orphanage in Kabul, the nation's capital, was given nearly five thousand pounds of school supplies, clothing, personal hygiene items and medical supplies from New York National Guard troops. The orphanage has nearly 350 boys, ages seven to seventeen.

"They know we're not here to hurt them, we're here to help them," Gallup said. "We're building infrastructure and improving security. I definitely feel like we have a ways to go, but I feel like we're making progress. I'd be willing to come back. We're doing a good job. There's a lot more work to do."

Jensen said that the most valuable lesson he's learned in Afghanistan is the teamwork needed to win a war, from frontline soldiers to people in finance, medical and personnel offices.

"Every piece has a part to play, and everyone's trying their best," he said.

We're here to root out the terrorists and build a nation that can stand on its own feet, police its own citizens and secure its own borders. We've found a lot of satisfaction in seeing progress in the short time we've been here. I believe there has been a difference.

MIKE BISS: POLICE CAPTAIN, PEACEKEEPER

Published May 11, 2008

The most important weapon in the war on terror can't be fired from a gun and won't explode on impact. The one thing that will win people over is hope and the promise of a better tomorrow; this is what U.S. troops in Afghanistan are giving this war-torn nation by building hospitals and schools and distributing basics, such as food and fuel needed for day-to-day survival.

Wilton's Mike Biss, a Saratoga Springs police captain, has just come back from Afghanistan, where he spent the past ten months training national police and army officers, a crucial part of helping the government there to stand on its own.

Saratoga Springs police captain Mike Biss had a life-changing tour of duty in Afghanistan with the Army National Guard.

"Change is the key," said Biss, fifty-three, a major in the Army National Guard.

Every kid we treat well over there is one less kid that grows up to be a terrorist. If we can help them to keep warm, go to school, help teachers and doctors to get more money, if we can show them there's hope, then we'll win. What do the other people promise them? More death and destruction.

The Biss family has a long history of military service. His uncle, also named Mike, was at D-Day, the Allied invasion of Normandy.

While most media attention is focused on Iraq, the struggle against insurgents and a deeply entrenched Taliban continues daily in Afghanistan, which has become America's "forgotten war." Biss was in harm's way on multiple occasions while out on patrol, narrowly escaping serious injury once from a roadside explosive device.

"There's a lot of guys doing a lot of good work over there, putting their neck on the line," he said.

In the months following September 11, 2001, U.S. and coalition forces drove the Taliban from power. Now, the government is slowly trying to establish order by sending trained military and police to each outlying province.

"The police did a lot of military missions," Biss said.

Not a day went by when four or five officers hadn't been killed. In some places, it's just like the Wild West. It's really hard to control. The country is barren; it's very mountainous, and most of the trees and vegetation have been stripped from years of warfare. Kabul, the capital, is just rubble. The air is filled with dust and debris. They burn everything—tires, feces—it's always hazy. You see kids begging and one-legged men hobbling around. The average lifespan is forty for a man.

However, because of the Taliban's influence, it's a male-dominated society. Women, for example, must wear a burqa, a head-to-toe covering with only a small opening for the eyes. It's one of several inescapable ironies in this ruggedly beautiful, yet tragic land.

"Ever since Alexander the Great, there's been fighting there," Biss said. "Afghanistan is at the crossroads of civilization between the Middle East and China."

But every morning, afternoon and night, he heard the prayers of faithful Muslims echoing through the mountains.

"Sometimes they'd have loudspeakers," he said. "It was kind of eerie at first."

One of Biss's most poignant encounters was with a little girl in an outlying village who was suffering from frostbite because she was barefoot. That's one instance where he was personally able to intervene and make a difference.

Returning home was both welcome and difficult, because of the friends and responsibilities he left behind.

"At night, I've found myself waking up, thinking of things I have to do," he said. "It's surreal being back here. I walked up and down the aisles at Walmart, looking at all the stuff, because over there there's nothing, no stores."

Biss retired from the National Guard in 2000, after twenty-eight years of service, but was recalled when the army put out a notice for retired officers with specialized skills. His civilian police work made him uniquely qualified for the training job in Afghanistan.

"I was actually pretty honored that they called me back," said Biss, who earned a Bronze Star.

Area by area, Afghani police officers were removed and sent to eight-week regional training centers, where they were subjected to rigorous ordeals. Only those most qualified returned to their former posts. When Biss arrived, for example, there were seventeen thousand Afghani national police officers because everyone wanted that kind of job. When he got done, there were just eight thousand, but those who passed the test were much more professional and able to handle the tasks at hand.

"I accomplished a lot," Biss said. "I see a difference. There's definitely been forward movement."

The pay grade has been increased, too, making Afghani officers want to do a better job.

Biss traveled all over the country, from Kunduz in the north to Kandahar in the south, absorbing the culture and climate.

"Chai, a green tea, is their favorite drink. We also had kabobs, but we don't know what kind of meat it was, probably lamb," Biss said. "It's considered rude if you don't take some."

Although half a world away now, the friendships Biss made will stay with him for the rest of his life. One was Wakil Ahmad, an Afghani police colonel, nicknamed "007" because of his affinity for James Bond movies.

"In everything we did, even though I was the one doing the training, we ran it by him first," Biss said.

It's all part of being a soldier and goodwill ambassador, both of which are needed in the ongoing battle, not just for this nation but in the hearts and minds of its people as well.

"If we can get it down to that lowest level, we'll win," Biss said. "It's going to take some time."

MIKE MAHONEY: BACK FROM AFGHANISTAN

Published January 24, 2009

BOCES instructor Mike Mahoney knows all about the battleground for the mind. That's why he's thrilled to be back after spending the past year in Afghanistan, where the Taliban assassinates teachers and children risk their lives to get an education.

Mahoney, an Army National Guard chief warrant officer, got a hero's welcome Friday morning as more than five hundred students and staff cheered him during a parade through the school, followed by ceremonies with state and local officials on hand.

"It's so important winning the hearts and minds of these people," he said. "These people don't want war. They want to have a life like we do. Go to school, have food on the table." All of these things are not wanted by the Taliban as it tries to destabilize the country and carry out its terrorist mission.

Army National Guard chief warrant officer Mike Mahoney got a warm reception from students and staff at Saratoga BOCES, where he teaches, upon returning home from Afghanistan.

Mahoney, fifty-five, of Ballston Spa, has been all over the world during a lengthy military career, starting out in the navy, where experiences ran the gamut, from picking up boat people off Vietnam to a support role during the Iran Hostage Crisis. His latest deployment was one of the most rewarding times of his life.

In Kuwait, where he stopped en route to Afghanistan and Kabul—the war-torn nation's capital—he was surprised to meet many of his former BOCES students who are now soldiers. On several occasions, one of them would yell out, "Hi, Mr. Mahoney!"

"It was great seeing these kids, but they weren't kids any more," he said.

> *They're doing a fantastic job defending their country, putting their lives on the line. They don't think twice about it. I was so proud to work with these people.*
>
> *Eighty percent of what we do over there is rebuilding the country's infrastructure—schools, telecommunications. The Afghan people have suffered horrible atrocities. There's poverty you wouldn't believe. The average person makes $400 per year, but they're some of the nicest people in the world. If they've got some food, they'll share it with you.*

Last fall, BOCES faculty and students, including a special education class taught by Mark Sullivan, sent more than a ton of school supplies to Mahoney for distribution to Afghan children. Each one got a backpack filled with pens, paper, notebooks and crayons.

"They were put in schools that had nothing," he said. "Under the Taliban, education was not allowed. They taught religion, but there was no basic reading, writing and arithmetic."

Goods were handed by out by the Afghan army as a way of building trust among children, in contrast to the Taliban that propagates ignorance and fear. Mahoney told about one girl who had acid thrown in her face just for attending school. Later, he saw a picture of her scars. With brave determination, she went back anyway.

"I was there, that's how it is," he said.

Things are kind of bad. There are lots of bad people in the world. Sometimes you have to take action to protect the good people. Our mission over there is security. We're doubling the number of troops. It's happening now. There are no immediate results in counter-insurgency warfare. You don't see the results until years later.

Students carried posters and banners as Mahoney, clad in full dress uniform, walked through the BOCES center's halls with a rendition of "Stars and Stripes" playing over the school's public address system. Posters were entered in a contest, with the winner getting a free pancake breakfast, compliments of the culinary arts classes.

"Hey Mike! Welcome back," teacher Dave Droddy called out. "Good to see you. Thanks for all you've done."

Public officials heaped lavish praise on Mahoney, including formal proclamations from the state assembly and senate and the U.S. Congress.

"It's men like Mr. Mahoney who inspire me to achieve my goals," said John Feulner, of Galway, a student in Mahoney's information technologies/computer networking class. He also thanked teacher Mike Williams for doing a good job during Mahoney's yearlong absence.

Mahoney returned home to the United States in late December and officially went back to work Thursday, following a vacation at St. Thomas in the Virgin Islands. Friday's celebration and outpouring of appreciation was more than he expected.

"It was just nice seeing people positive about patriotism," he said.

THREE GENERATIONS OF NAVY WOMEN

Published May 5, 2007

Pride runs deep in the Racht family, a natural byproduct for people with a history of military service. With Nicole Racht's recent boot camp graduation, the family can now boast the unusual feat of having three generations of navy women.

Racht, twenty-two, joins her mother, Connie, and grandmother, Esther, who were both on hand for the April 20 ceremonies at Great Lakes, Illinois, along with her father, Martyn, who had a twenty-year navy career, too.

"I was brought up to believe that if you can serve you should serve, and pride in that has always been instilled in me," she said. "I grew up watching my father serve every day, hearing about how the navy changed my mother's life, and finally I got to see my brother grow from an irritating boy to a man, almost overnight."

Nicole and her brother, David, both graduated from Saratoga Springs High School in 2003 and '04, respectively. He's currently a nuclear machinist mate, second class, aboard the submarine USS *Alexandria,* which returned from a seven-month Persian Gulf tour last November. The crew was more recently involved in joint polar ice cap exercises with the British navy.

"I have pride in my family," Nicole Racht said.

> *It makes us special with everything we've done in service to our country. I have pride in my country. I think we have the greatest nation and my family played a big part in that. I looked at my future and thought, "I can see myself regretting not doing this, but I can't see myself regretting it."*

The family's more than half century of navy service began with Nicole's grandparents, Robert and Esther Racht, in the early 1950s. He was a sonar technician on the USS *Darby,* a destroyer escort, toward the end of the Korean War. She was a hospital corpsman who worked in a Philadelphia naval hospital.

"I had a wonderful time," seventy-six-year-old Esther Racht said. "It was one of the greatest experiences. I hated to get out. I'd go back in today if I could."

Her lone regret is never going overseas, and she said she'd serve in Iraq if given the opportunity.

Connie Racht, forty-four, joined the navy when she was seventeen.

"It was basically just to get away from home," she said. "I was raised in Seattle and was ready to travel."

Like her mother-in-law, she spent most of her time on land, handling accounting duties in Groton, Connecticut. The lessons she learned have paid dividends the rest of her life.

"There's a great sense of accomplishment getting through boot camp," Connie Racht said. "It builds self-esteem, you learn how to get along with other people...and I met my husband."

Martyn Racht was a nuclear machinist mate, master chief, on three different subs, most recently with the USS *Providence*. His work brought him to the navy's West Milton nuclear facility, giving the family a chance to put down roots locally; they lived in Greenfield Center for twelve years beginning in 1994. He's since retired from the navy, and he and Connie now live in Avon, Indiana, where he's a pharmaceuticals industry consultant.

Nicole Racht said that she's glad to have boot camp behind her and admits that it wasn't easy.

"We showered every day, but we only had about seven minutes for the whole process, which is fun with forty females," she said.

> *We hit the racks at about 8:00 or 10:00 p.m. The most difficult part was learning how to push myself. Going from a life where I had very little personal responsibility to having people rely on me alone to get a job done is hard. Dealing with seventy-nine other people every day is hard, especially when half of them are females and there is zero privacy. Boot camp itself is not difficult. The real challenge is within yourself.*

When the going got tough, she said she turned her thoughts heavenward for extra reserves of strength.

"I pray a lot, almost constantly," she said. "I asked God to get me through this thing. I also tried to take everything in perspective, that it's not really that long."

Since graduating, she's moved into cryptology and is taking classes in Monterey, California.

"Language has always been something I'm good at, so it was just natural," she said. "As of right now, I'm in for life, but I really don't know how I'll feel in six years."

Of course, she also wants to see the world, with Japan and Australia high on her wish list. "Japan for the culture, Australia for the sightseeing," she said. "I want to live in Japan for a few years, and it's definitely a possibility."

Nicole's navy commitment might not be for life, but like other family members, it's been a life-changing experience.

ABOVE THE CALL
OF DUTY

MAJOR DAVID LAFRANCE: ANTARCTIC ICE RESCUE

Published November 28, 2008

Many service members put their lives on the line every day in noncombat situations. The following story is an example of the heroic deeds America's young men and women perform apart from the battlefield.

A Saratoga Springs man made national Australian news recently with the daring rescue of an injured expeditioner stranded in Antarctica for nearly two weeks.

Major David LaFrance has been flying mammoth, fifty-nine-ton C-130s to the South Pole for more than eleven years as a member of the 109th Airlift Wing, Air National Guard, in Scotia.

On November 4, while America was electing a new president, LaFrance was about as far from the United States as a person could be—flying to Davis Station on Antarctica, where resident chef Dwayne Rooke's life hung in the balance following an October 20 quad bike accident. Australia had to call on the United States for assistance because a ship bound for the site was blocked by heavy ice buildup.

"Down on the ice, every country works together," LaFrance said. "Based on the severity of the emergency, they look at the best possible option. There's been so much bad news lately with the economy and controversy over Iraq. It's nice to have something good happen. I was glad to be a part of it."

Major David LaFrance of Saratoga Springs flew a large C-130 to Antarctica for a daring ice rescue on November 4, 2008.

The flight crew included navigator Marc LeCours of Saratoga Springs and loadmaster Jamie Hill of Stillwater.

Normally, LaFrance lands at McMurdo Station, on Antarctica, and then makes daily flights to the South Pole or any number of deep field research stations. Davis Station was fifteen hundred miles away, on the opposite side of the frozen continent. More than the flight itself, LaFrance was concerned about the landing, with absolutely no ground-based instruments to assist him.

A team of workers using heavy equipment built a hastily made ten-thousand-foot-long runway on the ice.

"The biggest issue is that it's seasonal ice," LaFrance said. "It's not frozen year-round, and the water beneath it isn't deep. When you land, you don't want to create a wave beneath the ice that will crack it."

Australian scientists at Davis Station provided U.S. officials in Washington, D.C., with critical data—ice depth, temperatures—which they used to plan a successful landing. At touchdown, LaFrance had to make sure he didn't taxi too

Crew members and support personnel are dwarfed by the large C-130 that Major David LaFrance flew to Antarctica for a daring ice rescue.

fast or slow for fear of cracking the ice. All the while, he had to trust information supplied to him by complete strangers—from Australia and the United States.

Apprehensive?

"Absolutely," he said, without hesitation. "There were so many unknown variables. The runway was very, very slick. That was probably the slickest landing I've ever made."

Most takeoffs and landings in Antarctica are made on skis. This time, the C-130's huge tires were kept in place because of the ice. When landing, there's always a danger that one of the plane's propellers will shut down, causing the plane to slide sideways out of control. On snow, with more friction, LaFrance can compensate for those kinds of situations, while ice is much more dangerous. Fortunately, the threat didn't come into play as the aircraft and LaFrance performed to perfection.

"The biggest obstacle for us was making sure the penguins stayed out of our way," he told ABC News. People on the ground had to chase the large birds from the runway. If the plane hit them, they could get hung up in the landing gear and cause all kinds of problems."

"The Davis Station crew was well-prepared," LaFrance continued. "They did everything we needed. They even had big 155-gallon drums of fuel lined up waiting for us."

LaFrance was also interviewed by NBC's Australian Today Show, the nationwide Southern Cross Television and major Australian newspapers such as Sydney's *Morning Herald*.

Rooke had suffered two broken legs, a shattered pelvis and two broken ankles in the accident. The lone doctor at Davis Station had done his best, but Rooke required a blood transfusion and surgery and would have died without evacuation help from the United States.

Australian Antarctic Division director Tony Press told media:

> *I would like to thank our colleagues from the U.S. National Science Foundation, the U.S. Antarctic program and our friends from the U.S. Air Force. They have given us a great deal of assistance in getting Dwayne back to Australia. This effort underpins the spirit of cooperation of the Antarctic treaty and my staff have done a magnificent job.*

Following a mandatory rest period, LaFrance then took off for a twenty-six-hundred-mile flight to Tasmania, off the southern coast of Australia, where Rooke—who was sedated and immobilized for the trip—was treated at Royal Hobart Hospital. The medical rescue team consisted of an Australian doctor and nurse, three U.S. Army medical personnel and three U.S. Air Force medical personnel.

LaFrance flies twice-annual missions from Scotia to Antarctica, a five-day trip by way of Los Angeles, Hawaii, the U.S. Samoan islands and Christchurch, New Zealand. He learned about the rescue job while en route to Antarctica as part of a regular month-long deployment.

The rescue team was assembled in Christchurch and flew to McMurdo Station, where it had to wait three days for gale-force winds to subside.

"We're all down there together," LaFrance told the Sydney press. "It's nice, because everyone is concerned about the common man."

Originally from North Conway, New Hampshire, LaFrance is a talented athlete who competed in cross-country, downhill and ski-jumping events, made the Junior Olympics and graduated from the National Sports Academy in Lake Placid. Skiing took him to Steamboat Springs, Colorado, where he got a job handling luggage for Rocky Mountain Airways.

All he wanted was enough money to travel for skiing, but he got the chance one day to make a flight from inside the cockpit.

"It was just an adrenaline rush," he said. "That's where I got the flying bug."

With Air National Guard, he takes scientists to research stations throughout Antarctica.

"I'm flying some of the smartest people in the world who are studying things like global warming and ozone depletion," LaFrance said. "It's pretty rewarding to be a part of that."

Of course, there are drawbacks, too.

"Every job or profession I pick seems to take me to cold places," he said, laughing.

His wife, Andrea, would love to accompany LaFrance if his missions were to sunny Italy or Hawaii. "It's Antarctica, how jealous can you be?" she said, smiling. "One of these days I'd like to meet him in New Zealand."

USS SARATOGA

USS SARATOGA: GUARDIAN OF THE HIGH SEAS

Published July 25, 2009

Six different ships have been named USS *Saratoga* in American naval history, from a Revolutionary War–era sloop launched in 1780 to a modern aircraft carrier that took part in Desert Storm in the early 1990s.

The last ship was decommissioned at Mayport, Florida, on August 20, 1994, and is now docked at Newport, Rhode Island, where plans call for turning it into a living naval museum.

Many Saratoga County residents served aboard the fifth and sixth versions of the USS *Saratoga*. In 1998, its ship's bell was placed at Gerald B.H. Solomon Saratoga National Cemetery in Stillwater. In July 2009, ceremonies were held there honoring one-hundred-year-old John Finn, America's oldest living Medal of Honor recipient and the first to get the award from World War II. He served aboard the USS *Saratoga* before the war began.

Ceremonies honoring Finn were organized by USS *Saratoga* historian Larry Gordon of Wilton. Retired captain Douglas Dupouy of Greenfield, who served aboard the last USS *Saratoga*, rang the ship's bell. He was commanding officer of VF-74, a Tomcat squadron on the *Saratoga* during operations Desert Shield and Desert Storm in the early 1990s.

From 2000 to 2003, he was captain and commanding officer of the USS *Abraham Lincoln* (CVN-72), a nuclear-powered aircraft carrier.

The fifth USS *Saratoga* that Finn served aboard was originally planned as a battle cruiser but launched as a carrier, the world's first "modern floating airport." It was built at the New York Shipbuilding Co. in Camden, New Jersey, and christened with spring water from Saratoga Springs on April 7, 1925.

Before World War II, the USS *Saratoga* served as one of the first training and testing ships for the new science of naval aviation.

On December 4, 1941—Pearl Harbor Day—the ship was entering San Diego after an interim dry-docking and was immediately sent to the Pacific, carrying marine aircraft to the Midway Islands. The carrier suffered extensive damage during the war. It was struck twice by torpedoes and repaired twice in three years before suffering its most serious damage on February 21, 1945, during the invasion of Iwo Jima.

During that encounter, five Japanese suicide planes and seven bombs struck the ship, killing 123 men, wounding 192 and causing extensive structural damage.

The USS *Saratoga* earned nine battle stars before the war was over. During its seventeen years, the USS *Saratoga* was the site of 98,549 plane landings, a record for the most landings on a carrier. After the Japanese surrender, it joined the Magic Carpet Fleet, bringing home 29,204 veterans, more than any other ship.

In 1946, the fifth USS *Saratoga* was officially decommissioned when it was sunk as part of an atomic bomb test at Bikini Atoll in the South Pacific. It was replaced by the sixth and latest ship, also an aircraft carrier.

Former Saratoga County treasurer George Gasser of Saratoga Springs had four separate stints aboard this ship with the navy reserves. His last duty was in 1994, during the conflict in Bosnia, shortly before the ship's decommissioning.

"I was on the last cruise," Gasser said. "I spent most of my time on submarines. When I went on the *Saratoga* I was amazed at how a huge machine like that, with five thousand people, could work so intricately. It changed my opinion of surface ships."

Commander Jack Eckert, of Saratoga Springs, served on the *Saratoga* in the early 1960s. He was the first to ring the ship's bell at ceremonies honoring Finn. The bell was rung twenty-one times, similar to a twenty-one-gun salute. Twenty-one is the sum of the numerals 1776.

Frank Klementowski, of Saratoga Springs, was on the *Saratoga* from 1956 to 1958 as a second-class electrician. He recalled a funny incident in Brooklyn at the end of a "shakedown" cruise when the ship was first put into service.

"We dropped anchor and it kept going, right to the bottom," he said. "Each link in the chain weighed 360 pounds, and the anchor was thirty tons. After that they put a braking system on it."

One of the most interesting stories about the *Saratoga* deals with a voyage it once made to Greece. While there, sailors went ashore, and three of them befriended a young man named John Kontos. Later, when Kontos immigrated to the United States, he didn't know where to go and chose Saratoga Springs because of the friends he made aboard the USS *Saratoga*.

Eventually, he founded the Spa City Diner on South Broadway. Years later, about sixty shipmates held a reunion in Saratoga Springs, and twenty-two members of the Kontos family stood outside the diner, waving to sailors as they rode by in a bus. A large banner adorned the diner, too, welcoming crew members.

"Whenever anyone from the USS *Saratoga* visited his diner, there was no charge," Gasser said. "He always treated them very well."

Following is a brief description of each of the USS *Saratoga* ships— three sailing ships (Revolution, War of 1812, Civil War) an armored cruiser and two aircraft carriers that served in World War II and Desert Storm, respectively.

1. A sloop, built in Philadelphia by Warton and Humphries, it was begun in December 1779 and launched on April 10, 1780. It vanished at sea in March 1781.

2. Launched on April 11, 1814, on Lake Champlain, it played a major role in the Battle of Plattsburgh, a pivotal American victory during latter stages of the War of 1812. It was laid up and sold in Whitehall, New York, in 1825.

3. A sloop of war launched at the Portsmouth (New Hampshire) Navy Yard on July 26, 1842, it was commissioned on January 4, 1843. On April 21, 1861, it captured the slave ship *Nightengale* off Kabenda, Africa, freeing a cargo of numerous slaves. At the outbreak of the Civil War, it returned to the United States and was decommissioned in Philadelphia on August 25, 1861.

4. Launched from the William Cramp and Sons Shipyard in Philadelphia on December 2, 1891, it was first the armored cruiser USS *New York*. It was renamed USS *Saratoga* on February 16, 1911, when it was the flagship of the Asiatic Station. On the eve of America's entry into World War I, it was renamed again to USS *Rochester* and served as an escort ship during the war. It was decommissioned in the Philippines on April 29, 1933, and deliberately sunk in the Subic Channel on Christmas Eve 1941 to prevent its capture by the Japanese.

5. *Saratoga* (CV-3) was laid down on September 25, 1920, as Battle Cruiser No. 3 by the New York Shipbuilding Co. in Camden, New Jersey. It was

reclassified as an aircraft carrier in 1922 and launched on April 7, 1925, the first fast carrier in the United States Navy.

6. The most modern *Saratoga* was laid down on December 16, 1952, by the New York Naval Shipyard in New York, launched on October 8, 1955, and commissioned on April 14, 1956. It was decommissioned at Mayport, Florida, on August 20, 1994.

EPILOGUE

There is virtually no end to the stories that could be included in *Soldiers of Saratoga County*, so finding a good ending was one of the most challenging tasks of completing this project. The Civil War section included a story about the unknown soldier from Antietam whose remains were reinterred at Saratoga National Cemetery in September 2009. I wrote the following brief essay at that time and could think of no more fitting conclusion to this book.

HOME AT LAST

Published September 18, 2009

He might have come from a New York tenement, a small upstate mill town or a rural farm family. No one knows for sure.

In the end, his name and address are mere footnotes.

What matters are the things he died fighting for, and the soldier laid to rest Thursday at Saratoga National Cemetery would be proud to know that a century and a half later he made a difference and that many people still think so. A crowd of more than 500, including 130 Schuylerville eighth graders, turned out for the unknown Civil War soldier's interment on the 147th anniversary of the Battle of Antietam, where he made the ultimate sacrifice on September 17, 1862.

"Can you imagine?" said Bob Fickies of Averill Park. "There was no radio, no TV back then. If a genie told him 150 years ago this was going to be happening to him, he'd have no concept."

The unknown Civil War soldier, killed at Antietam, comes home at last.

Indeed, a lot has changed. In 1862, millions of African Americans were still living under the bondage of slavery, and President Lincoln wouldn't issue the Emancipation Proclamation until early the next year.

On Monday, President Barack Obama is scheduled to talk about the economy at Hudson Valley Community College in Troy.

Fickies had two great-grandfathers who fought in the War Between the States. "This is history we're looking at," he said, as the black nineteenth-century hearse carrying the soldier's remains rolled by.

Shortly after Antietam, where twenty-three thousand men were killed or wounded during twelve hours of fighting, the dead were buried in shallow graves. Most were reinterred after the war at Antietam National Cemetery. Somehow, one seventeen- to nineteen-year-old soldier was overlooked and left forgotten until last October, when a hiker stumbled across bone fragments and uniform buttons, which identified him as being from New York.

"He was lost for but a moment but is now returned home," said Chaplain Eric Olsen of the New York State Division of Military and Naval Affairs. "He stood shoulder to shoulder in horrible conditions. He fought death and disease on a daily basis. It is such soldiers that have made our nation great."

Had his body been found and buried at Antietam, it's doubtful that many loved ones would have showed up. In the mid-nineteenth century, Maryland was an expensive several days' journey from New York.

"This turnout is just amazing," said Ron Graham, a Vietnam veteran from Fort Edward. "It's good to see young people here, too. My great-grandfather, William Reynolds, was with the 123rd Queensbury Volunteer Regiment. He served from 1862 to '65. I have his discharge papers home."

The unknown Union soldier died in a section of the battlefield called Miller's Cornfield. Did he see his assailant? Was he shot from behind or in front? Or did he succumb to something even more vicious, a bayonet wound?

"We do know this about our men and women in uniform," said Major General Joseph Taluto, adjutant general for the New York National Guard. "They are patriots. They are loyal to their country and comrades. They are selfless in their service. They have integrity and courage. That's what we know about this soldier."

Now, for all time, he will rest at section 7, site 124 of the cemetery, given a special place of honor separate from the long rows of granite headstones marking more than eight thousand other graves.

"Right here under these trees," said Paul Lyman, a cemetery official.

As the soldier's pine casket was lowered into the ground, someone called out, "God bless America!"

"Amen!" the crowd responded in unison.

Some things, thank goodness, don't change, while other things that should change never do.

"Maybe someday there won't have to be any more of these," said Joseph Bilello, a veteran from Croton.

"That would be nice," said a fellow onlooker, Mavourneen Roy, of Troy.

God bless our troops. God bless the USA.

Appendix

CONTENTS BY TOWNSHIP

SARATOGA COUNTY

WARREN COUNTY

WASHINGTON COUNTY

ABOUT THE AUTHOR

Paul Post has been in the newspaper field for thirty years, the past fifteen with *The Saratogian* in Saratoga Springs, New York, where he has won numerous state and national writing awards. His November 2008 three-part series on veterans won first place in the Suburban Newspapers of America national feature-writing contest. Those stories and the subjects he profiled—Morris Katz (World War II), Bob Nevins (Vietnam) and Mike Biss (Afghanistan)—are contained in *Soldiers of Saratoga County*, the author's third book.

His other works are *The Never Ending Story, What's Fit to Print: The Life of Harness Racing Legend Harold Story* and *Foresight 20/20: The Life of Major League Baseball Scout Ralph DiLullo.*

Mr. Post has also written more than five hundred magazine articles for several dozen magazines, primarily sports related. He is a frequent contributor to *Baseball Digest, Sports Collector's Digest* and *Baseball America* and has written for a variety of environmental, public policy, travel and trade publications.

He lives in Glens Falls, New York, and enjoys sports, travel and history.

Visit us at
www.historypress.net